PowerPoint® 2003
for Professors

EasyTech Series

PowerPoint® 2003 for Professors

Deanne C. Siemer

Frank D. Rothschild

Paul J. Zwier

National Institute for Trial Advocacy

Reproduction Permission
National Institute for Trial Advocacy
361 Centennial Parkway, Suite 220
Louisville, CO 80027
(800) 225-6482
Web site: www.nita.org

Siemer, Deanne C., Frank D. Rothschild, Paul J. Zwier, *PowerPoint 2003 for Professors* (NITA 2007).

ISBN 978-1-55681-980-3

Library of Congress Cataloging-in-Publication Data

Siemer, Deanne C.
  PowerPoint 2003 for professors / Deanne C. Siemer, Frank D. Rothschild, Paul J. Zwier.
    p. cm. -- (EasyTech series)
  ISBN 978-1-55681-980-3 (pbk. : alk. paper) 1. Presentation graphics software. 2. Microsoft PowerPoint (Computer file) 3. Teaching--Aids and devices. 4. Teachers--In-service training. I. Rothschild, Frank D., 1944- II. Zwier, Paul J., 1954- III. Title.
T385.S5135 2007

005.5'8--dc22   2007020430

TABLE OF CONTENTS

ACKNOWLEDGMENTS

The authors taught the first experimental course in PowerPoint for Professors at Southern High School in Saipan, CNMI, and we are grateful to the thirty-five college and high school teachers who attended that course for their constructive suggestions. We have drawn from the innovative work by Sam Solomon and his talented colleagues at DOAR Communications with respect to this book and others in the EasyTech series. Our particular thanks to Christopher Contois at DOAR, who helped with shortcuts he had devised and helped improve those that we used. The authors are also indebted to everyone who worked on *PowerPoint for Litigators* (NITA 2000) and *PowerPoint 2002 for Litigators* (NITA 2002), from which some of the materials in this book were taken.

The editing on this book was done by Ashley Smith. The page design and cover design were done by Judith Phillips, and the authors thank both of them for their great work.

ABOUT THE AUTHORS

Deanne C. Siemer is a Managing Director of Wilsie Co. LLC, a consulting firm located in Washington, D.C., which provides strategy advice to corporate and nonprofit clients. She has been a partner at a large Washington law firm where she specialized in commercial jury trial cases in federal and state courts. She serves as a court-appointed arbitrator and mediator and teaches courses in trial practice and courtroom technology.

Frank D. Rothschild is a judge in Kauai, Hawaii, and serves professionally as a mediator and arbitrator. He was a trial lawyer on civil cases in private practice and was appointed as a public defender and state prosecutor handling criminal cases. He teaches courses in trial practice and courtroom technology and provides training for

judges and law firms. He also provides PowerPoint slide design services and consults on cases.

Paul J. Zwier is a professor at Emory University School of Law where he directs the trial advocacy and litigation skills programs and also teaches torts and an advanced negotiation and mediation seminar. He is the Director of Education for the National Institute for Trial Advocacy and specializes in designing learning-by-doing programming for teaching advanced legal skills. He also consults on ADR strategies as well as case theory and presentation in trial cases.

INTRODUCTION

Many of us are visual learners; 60 to 80 percent of us like to learn by seeing pictures, diagrams, flow charts, and time lines. We can, of course, learn by listening, especially if the lecturer uses words like *see*, or *imagine*, or *picture this*. However, most of us do not like lectures unassisted by pictures that go on for too long. At the same time, visual learners are easily distracted by movement and untidiness. In fact, studies show that PowerPoint-assisted learning can be memorable for its presentation and movement at the cost of memory of the content.

Other types of learners can also benefit from Power-Point. Sequential learners can be shown information in steps and ordering that can enhance their understanding. Global learners can be shown the big picture before getting into the detail. Even sensing learners are assisted by seeing the structure of what they are about to learn, and intuitive learners are helped by seeing relationships between ideas and thrive on comparisons and abstract connections between ideas.

The common use of technology in games and media, and as a way to receive information, has only fed the students' expectation, that visuals will accompany our lectures and presentations. Teachers need to use well-crafted visuals that will enhance, rather than detract from, the learning process.

Beginners and experienced computer users will find this book useful because it is focused specifically on designing and constructing the most common kinds of enlarged displays for use in teaching.

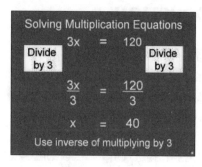

A free-form slide using various sized boxes that can be moved around the screen works well for science, math, and similar formula-based concepts. Chapter 2 explains how to design and construct these slides.

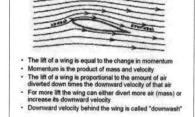

A structured slide containing an outline or list of points helps display the logic of your presentation and the facts that support your themes. Chapter 3 contains instructions for creating these slides.

Teachers in many subject matter areas can make good use of photos, maps, drawings, and other illustrations. Chapter 4 explains how to put scanned images on a slide and enhance the image to make important points.

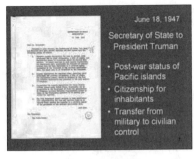

June 18, 1947

Secretary of State to
President Truman

- Post-war status of
  Pacific islands
- Citizenship for
  inhabitants
- Transfer from
  military to civilian
  control

History and literature lectures can be enhanced with the actual documents on a projection screen so that all the students in the class are following the discussion. Chapter 5 has directions for making this kind of slide.

Creating slides is not difficult and does not require any computer experience. Each chapter tells you what you are going to do, gives an overview of the steps necessary to get there, and guides you through the process one logical step at a time. Chapter 7 describes how to make and publish teaching notes about your slides. Chapter 8 contains tips on making presentations in a classroom supported by a slide show. Chapter 9 provides a refresher on basic Windows and PowerPoint vocabulary and tools and describes the hardware and software that you need to use this book.

This book focuses on PowerPoint 2003, which is very similar to PowerPoint 2002. If you have an earlier version, consider downloading an upgrade, which is easy and inexpensive to do. The basic instructions provided in this book are supplemented in the book *PowerPoint 2003: 50 Great Tips for Better, Easier Slides* (NITA 2005) which provides shortcuts and additional slide construction ideas.

With these techniques the PowerPoint slide can become your easel and canvas to help your students regardless of their learning styles and preferences. You can help the *visual learner* see it, the *intuitive* and *global* learner get the big picture and understand relationships between ideas and concepts, the *sensor* understand the steps and sequence, and all of us understand and remember the key facts and causal relationships no matter the complexity of the subject matter or the abstractness of the learning.

STARTER SLIDES

To help you get going quickly in making your slides, a download is available at http://www.nita.org/pp4profs. It contains full-color and animated versions of all of the slides in this book.

With the downloaded starter slides on your computer you can—

- ✓ Copy a starter slide that has a design you would like to use.

- ✓ Paste the starter slide into the slide show to accompany your lecture.

- ✓ Change the words on the slide to the subject matter you are teaching.

- ✓ Change the colors on the slide—the background, the fill in the boxes on the slide, and the color of the lettering.

- ✓ Check out the animation that is provided and change it if you want.

The starter slides provide the layout and design. You provide the content.

Get your slide show put together in half the time.

Chapter 1
Basic PowerPoint Moves
for Educational Slides

Educators have always used creative materials to illustrate lectures. Illustrations help make a clearer presentation, assist in sequencing the learning, control where the learner is looking, and add emphasis to important points. Creating illustrative materials also helps the educator become better prepared.

PowerPoint provides a way to use text, photos, drawings, color, font, underlining, and all of the kinds of things an educator would do on a blackboard or whiteboard. The software is reliable and easy to use, and the techniques for most kinds of educational slides are remarkably consistent.

Four moves are used in creating nearly all educational slides—create a blank slide, color the background, put something onto the blank slide (a rectangle, circle, photo, or document), and work with the layout of the slide by adjusting the size of the things you have put on the slide and moving them around on the slide. In addition, there are three editing techniques that make the work go much faster: these allow you to duplicate things, delete things, and "undo" mistakes. The basics also include opening, closing, and saving the file on which you are working and entering and exiting the software.

This chapter covers these basics in the context of creating a "black slide" that goes at the beginning and end of every educational slide show. When you are using your computer in a classroom, you want it to wait silently, with nothing visible on the screen, until you are ready to go. At that instant, you want the slide show to come alive with the first slide without any distraction between the point you are making orally and the first point you make visually. This is accomplished by using a black slide as the first slide in the show. The black slide presents a blank screen although, in reality, the computer is projecting the black slide.

Black slides are also used in the middle of a slide show to "blank" the screen. When the screen is dark, students' attention is focused on the instructor. Similarly, at the end of a slide show, perhaps near the end of your class, you want the screen to show no image at all so you can move to the concluding points in the discussion with the focus solely on you.

If you have never used PowerPoint or use it only infrequently, you may want to consult Chapter 9, which contains explanations of basic terminology, instructions for working on advanced slides, and a short refresher on PowerPoint controls. Everything you need to know to make effective educational slides is covered in this book.

1.1 Create a blank slide

A blank slide is the starting point for many kinds of educational slides. PowerPoint has a large number of preformatted layouts, but most do not work well in a classroom. The blank slide will permit you to tailor all of the details for your particular classroom situation. Follow the three easy steps described below.

A. Check to be sure the Task Pane is showing.

If PowerPoint is not already running on your computer when you start to work, turn it on. Follow the instructions in section 9.2(B).

The Task Pane is a generic name for the panel located along the right side of the screen. If the Task Pane is not there, restore it. See directions in section 9.2(D) (1).

When the Task Pane first appears, it generally looks like this. The title bar on the Task Pane says "Getting Started." There is a small down arrow to the right of the title for access to the menu of panes that can be displayed in this space. There is also an "X" for deleting the pane altogether.

B. Go to the New Presentation Pane.

The Task Pane houses the New Presentation Pane. Click on the down arrow key immediately to the right of Getting Started. A drop-down menu will appear. Click on the New Presentation option. The New Presentation Pane looks like this.

The New Presentation Pane has four options for starting work on your slide show.

Blank presentation: Create a new slide show from scratch.

From design template: Start with a template that comes with the software. A template is a basic design for a slide, complete with colors and typeface choices provided by the software. Most templates provided by the software or Web sites are geared toward sales and marketing presentations. They limit options in slide design and contain defaults that are difficult to override. They are not recommended.

From AutoContent wizard: Start from a series of instructions that provide content suggestions as well as a template.

From existing presentation: This option allows you to start with a slide show that you already have on your computer so that you can modify it for your current purposes.

For educational slides, you will likely use only the first and last of these options. Commercial templates (option 2) usually do not work well in the classroom, and the AutoContent wizard (option 3) offers help for general business purposes.

When you get to the New Presentation Pane, look at the very bottom. The small box at the bottom-left corner labeled "Show when inserting new slides" should be checked. If it is not, click to check it. This brings the Slide Layout Pane to the screen automatically when the New Slide button is used. See section 2.1.

C. Open a Blank Presentation.

1. Click on the Blank Presentation option.

The Task Pane will switch automatically to the Slide Layout Pane. Now the Task Pane looks like the illustration on the right.

The Slide Layout Pane displays four category headings: Text Layouts, Content Layouts, Text and Content Layouts, and Other Layouts. Nearly all educational slides will use just three of these many options: the Title Only layout (top row, right), the Title and Text layout (second row, left), or the Blank Slide layout (third row, left).

2. Click on the Blank layout.

The display in the middle of your screen will change to a blank slide format. You are now ready to create slides.

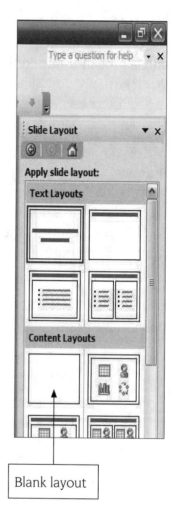

Blank layout

1.2 Color a slide

The "background" of a slide is the whole area of the slide behind anything like photos or shapes that you put on the slide. The term background usually refers to color.

A. Open the Background dialog box.

1. Go to the Formatting toolbar.

This toolbar is at the top of your screen and contains these buttons with which you are familiar from word processing work.

It is easier to use the Formatting toolbar if you have located it *below* the Standard toolbar, and if you have displayed all of its buttons. Sometimes when PowerPoint is loaded onto a computer, it displays the Formatting toolbar on the same level (and to the right of) the Standard toolbar containing these buttons with which you are also familiar from word processing work.

You can move it to the level below the Standard toolbar following the directions in section 9.2(E)(4). If the Formatting toolbar is on the same level as the Standard toolbar, it won't have enough room to display *all* of its buttons, so some buttons are hidden and the Background button will be among those that are hidden. You can display all of the necessary buttons by following the directions in section 9.2(E)(5).

2. Click on the Background button.

 This button is at the far right end of the For-matting toolbar. It looks like a spilling paint can. The Background dialog box appears in the middle of the slide on which you are working. It looks like this:

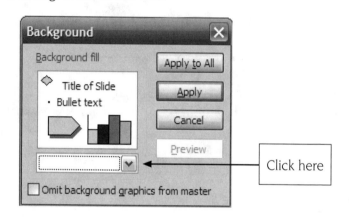

B. Designate the color.

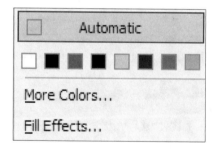

1. Click on the small down arrow in the Background dialog box next to the box indicating the current color choice. (Note: the blank slide has a white background, so the box shows a white color.) A second dialog box appears.

2. Click on the small box representing black. The Background dialog box will now show your choice—a black background—so you can check to see if it is what you want.

3. Click on the Apply button (*not* the Apply to All button) on the Background dialog box. Your slide will now be colored black. (Had you selected the Apply to All button, each succeeding slide would start off with a black background.)

1.3 Duplicate a slide

It is often useful to create duplicates of slides because the duplicate will contain all of the formatting and design work you have done on the original. This saves considerable time. To duplicate a slide, follow these steps.

A. Activate the thumbnail of the slide.

1. Go to the Slides Pane.

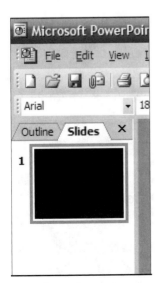

This is the panel on the left edge of the screen that shows thumbnails (or miniature versions) of your slides as you create them. It looks like this.

If the Slides Pane is not displayed, restore it. See section 9.2(D)(1). If the Slides Pane is displayed but no thumbnails are showing, click on the tab labeled "Slides" at the top of the pane.

2. Click on the thumbnail of the black slide. A blue border will appear around the thumbnail indicating that it is "active."

B. Use the CTRL+D control.

Hold down the CTRL key on your keyboard and press the D key at the same time. A duplicate slide will appear on your Slides Pane.

The blue border is now around this slide, as it is in the one that is active. You now have two black slides—one for the beginning of the show and one for the end of the show.

1.4 Delete a slide

You may want to take a slide out of a slide show if you have decided that it does not work or is not needed.

Delete one of the black slides just for practice—

A. Activate the thumbnail of the slide.

1. Go to the Slides Pane (the panel on the left edge, shown in the illustration in section 1.3(A)).

2. Click on the thumbnail of the slide to be deleted. A blue border will appear around the slide indicating that it is active.

B. Use the DELETE key on the keyboard.

Press the delete key once. The slide will disappear from the Slides Pane and has been deleted from the slide show.

Alternatively, with the thumbnail active—blue border showing—you can *right* click with your mouse and select the Delete Slide option from the menu that appears.

1.5 Put a box on the slide

When you are using a black slide at the beginning of a PowerPoint presentation, it is very useful to have a small box on the slide to signal to you that the computer and projector are working properly. The black slide shows nothing on the screen except a small colored square in the lower-right corner. The rest of the screen appears blank although, in reality, the computer is projecting the black slide. If the little square disappears, you know you have trouble and you need to check either the projector or the computer. For help in troubleshooting, see *The Digital Projector and Laptop Computer*, Chapter 11 (NITA 2005).

To put a box on the slide, do this—

A. Activate the rectangle (box) control.

1. Go to the Drawing toolbar at the bottom of the screen. See illustration in section 9.2(C)(2).

 2. Click on the Rectangle button. It looks like the illustration to the left. This creates a box that can be placed anywhere on the slide.

B. Place the box on the slide.

1. Move your mouse pointer toward the lower right corner of your slide.

2. Click once at the location you have chosen. A small box appears on your slide.

You are now ready to change the size or location of the box, color it, provide it with a line border, or duplicate it. Each of these operations is described below. Your slide now looks like this.

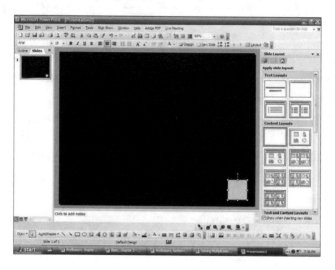

1.6 Improve the layout of the slide

In this case, you would want your signal to be a very small box, usually in the lower right corner (but also appropriate at any other location you like), noticeable only to you. The rectangle button puts a standard sized box on the screen that is a one-inch square. You can improve the layout of the slide by resizing the box and moving the box to the correct location. This section also covers duplicating, rotating, and deleting a box.

A. Resize the box.

Every box (and every other kind of "object" you use in PowerPoint) has "handles" on it, and you can use these handles to resize. See section 9.3(D) on handles.

You can make the box wider or narrower with the middle handles that show up as small circles in the left and right borders of the box.

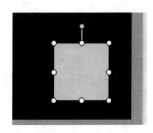

You can make the box taller or shorter with the middle handles that are in the top and bottom borders of the box.

You can change both the height and width at the same time using the corner handles on the box.

1. Make sure the box is active.

The box must be active (border and handles showing) in order to resize it. Click on it if it is not active and the handles will appear.

2. Position the mouse pointer over a handle.

Decide which handle to use. Position your mouse pointer over one of the handles. The mouse pointer shape will change from an arrow with one point to an arrow with two points, one at each end.

3. Drag the handle.

Hold down the left mouse button. Drag the handle outward to increase the size of the box, or inward to decrease the size of the box. Use a box that is small enough not to be noticed readily by the students but that is easily visible to you.

Release the left mouse button when the box is the desired size.

If the initial resizing does not accomplish exactly what you want, resize again. You can use the handles as many times as necessary.

B. Move the box.

On a black slide, the colored signal box should be un-obtrusive, so you may want to locate the box closer to the margin of the slide, or to the left or right of the location where you initially put it.

Any rectangle that is active (handles showing) can be moved. There are three ways to move a rectangle box—across a relatively large space, across a relatively small space, and across a very small space.

1. Make large moves.

   ✓ Move your mouse pointer over the box. The mouse pointer will change to a four-arrow shape. See illustration in section 9.3(B)(2).

   ✓ Hold down the left mouse button and drag the box to a new location. Let up on the mouse button when the box is where you want it.

2. Make small moves.

   ✓ Press one of the directional ARROW keys on the keyboard. This moves the box in relatively small increments in the direction indicated by the arrow.

   ✓ If you hold down the ARROW key, the object will keep moving in small increments.

3. Make very small moves.

   ✓ Hold down the CTRL key on the keyboard.

✓ Press one of the directional ARROW keys on the keyboard. This moves the box in very small increments in the direction indicated by the arrow.

C. Duplicate a box.

Just for practice, duplicate the small signal box this way—

✓ Hold down the CTRL key on the keyboard.

✓ Press the D key. A duplicate box will appear just below and to the right of the original box.

You can now move the duplicate box to another location on the slide. See section B.

To create a second duplicate, use the CTRL+D control again.

The CTRL+D keys will duplicate any object—a photo, document, rectangle, line, or oval.

D. Rotate a box.

The rectangle (and many other PowerPoint objects) has a Rotate handle that can be used to turn the box in either direction.

Just for practice, turn the box 90 degrees so that it rests on its side. The box must be active (border and handles showing) in order to rotate it.

The Rotate handle is a small green dot sitting just above the top of the box. If the green dot is not showing, enlarge the text box a little more, and it will appear.

✓ Move your mouse pointer to the green dot and hover there until the mouse pointer changes shape and becomes a circle.

✓ Hold the left mouse button down and drag the Rotate handle in a clockwise direction. The box will turn in the direction you drag the handle.

E. Delete a box.

Just for practice, delete the duplicate box that you have created.

✓ Activate the duplicate box.

✓ Press the DELETE key on the keyboard. (Alternatively, *right* click on the box and select the Cut option from the menu that appears.) The duplicate box will disappear.

1.7 "Undo" a mistake

You may make a move in working on your slides that turns out to be a mistake. For example, you may accidentally delete something you have spent quite a long time creating. The marvelous Undo button on the Standard toolbar allows you to backtrack to recapture your work as it was before you made the mistake.

 To "undo" the operation that you just completed in subsection E above, go to the Standard toolbar at the top of your screen and click on the Undo button, which looks like the illustration at the left. The box that you deleted will reappear on the screen.

Each click on the button will take you back one move. So, for example, if you click again, the Undo button will remove the rotation that you did in subsection D, and if you click again, the Undo button will remove the duplicate box that you made in subsection C. The small down arrow to the right of the Undo button lists the moves that can be undone.

If you go too far and undo more than you intended, the next-door button is the "redo" feature that takes you forward one step at a time.

PowerPoint is usually set to "undo" twenty moves. You can increase this to fifty or more. See instructions in section 9.2(F).

1.8 Save your work

It is very important to save your work often. Glitches happen and can cause you to lose slides or entire slide shows if they have not been saved.

A. Open the Save As dialog box.

1. Go to the Standard Toolbar.

2. Click on the Save button.

 The button looks like the illustration to the left, with a floppy disk (which used to be the principal means of saving files) on it.

When you save your work on a particular slide show for the first time, PowerPoint delivers the Save As dialog box that asks you to name the file. When you save this file on subsequent occasions, the Save button operates automatically. The dialog box looks something like this on the following page, depending on how your computer is set up and the folders it contains.

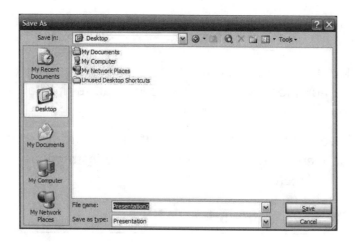

B. Create a folder for your slides.

1. Go to the Save In box at the top of the dialog box.

When you first go to the Save As dialog box, the Save In box usually displays the location called "Desktop."

That is the most general location that your computer has. It is the very first screen that appears when you turn your computer on. You can accept this location or change it. It is not a good idea to store all your files on the desktop because that screen will become cluttered.

2. Select the "My Documents" folder.

The Save As dialog box offers you a general alternative, which is the "My Documents" folder. That is a general storage place, and a good choice when you are starting out because the "My Documents" choice appears on the screen in almost every view, so you can always get back there.

Click on the icon called "My Documents" in the panel on the left side of the dialog box. "My Documents" will now appear in the Save In box at the top of the dialog box.

3. Create a new folder within "My Documents."

A folder is a software device that organizes files. Some folders are already created when you start up the computer for the first time. The "My Documents" folder is this kind of ready-made folder. (Depending on which operating system you are using, other ready-made folders may appear such as "My Pictures," "My Music," and "My Broadcasts.")

Any folder can hold just files, or it can also hold a number of other folders if you want to organize your files further. To create a folder for your slide shows, within your "My Documents" folder, do this—

✓Go to the toolbar at the top of the Save As dialog box. It looks like this.

✓Click on the New Folder button. A small dialog box will appear.

✓Type the name for the folder in the dialog box.

✓Click on the OK button. The name of the new folder will now be in the "Save In" box on the toolbar. Now you can save the PowerPoint file you are working on, and it will be put in the new folder.

When you click on the "My Documents" folder, it will display the new folder you have just created.

C. Designate a name for the file.

1. Go to the File Name box at the bottom left of the Save As dialog box which is still on your screen.

2. Choose a short name for this slide show.

3. Type the name into the File Name box.

D. Designate a file type.

Look here

The file "type" is the format which the software uses to store the file. There are several available formats, each of which serves a special purpose.

In the Save As dialog box, below the File Name box, you will see the Save As Type box.

"Presentation" is the choice that should be showing. That is the right choice for working with PowerPoint slides. If something else is showing, click on the arrow at the right side of the box to display a drop-down menu and pick the Presentation option.

E. Save the file.

Click on the Save button at the lower right. This completes the process.

It is important to save your work early and often during the process of constructing slides. A lot of time-consuming work can be lost to computer crashes. Your computer can take care of this for you with its Auto-Save function that saves at regular intervals. Lower the AutoSave time to 1 minute. See section 9.2(F).

1.9 Close, exit, and reopen the program

A. Close the file.

1. Go to the Menu Bar. This is the toolbar just under the blue bar at the very top of the screen. The buttons on the Menu Bar all have written names (File, Edit, View) rather than icons.

2. Click on the File button. A drop-down menu will appear.

3. Click on the Close option.

4. If you have made any changes since you last saved the file, PowerPoint will ask you if you want to save these changes before exiting the program. Choose yes to save the file, or no to discard the changes. This will close the file you are working on, but PowerPoint will still be running.

B. Exit the program.

1. Go to the Menu Bar.

2. Click on the File button. A drop-down menu will appear.

3. Click on the Exit option at the very bottom of the menu.

C. Reopen the program.

This is the same series of steps as shown in section 9.3(B).

D. Reopen the file.

1. Go to the Standard Toolbar.

2. Click on the Open button. (It is a yellow file folder, usually the second button from the left.) The Open dialog box will appear.

3. Click on the small down arrow to the right of the "Look in" box at the top of the dialog box. This will display the directory structure on your computer.

4. Click on the My Documents folder. This will open the folder and display its contents.

5. Click on the name of the file containing your PowerPoint presentation. This will open the file and display the first slide on your screen.

E. Run the slide show.

For instructions on how to run the slide show once you have created it, see section 8.2.

Chapter 2
Box Displays for Math,
Science, and Language

PowerPoint provides an easy way to teach math and science formulae, principles, rules, or laws. It helps sequence the information, facts, words, or variables the students must consider and helps them understand the order of operations and steps needed to solve a problem. It also permits side by side comparisons for showing the relationship between two ideas, helping intuitive learners with their need to see the big picture. In addition, adding a boxed heading keeps the big picture in mind and provides a continual context for the learning.

For example, you can display each part of a math formula or series of formulae as you explain how to work with the underlying concept. Other sample slides for different academic subjects are set out at the end of this chapter. All of these slides are made the same way.

Suppose, as in the illustration above, that you were teaching algebra and you wanted to illustrate the principles involved in solving multiplication equations. You want to show that each side of the equation has to remain equal, and that the equation is solved by using the inverse of multiplying.

This slide shows the basic operations and, using PowerPoint's animation capability, you can make each part of the slide appear separately as you explain. Then you can e-mail the slides to your students or post them on a Web site or server for downloading to ensure that their notes about your explanation are correct.

The steps for making the sample slide shown above are described in detail in this chapter. Once you have made the first such slide, it can be used as a template for other similar slides or you can use the principles illustrated here to create almost any kind of slide with text and numbers.

In this chapter, you will be changing some of the attributes of the boxes and text in order to build the sample slide. The *default* attributes (like color, size, style) are those that the software uses if it is not told to use something else. For example, the *default* background color for a slide is white. In Chapter 1, you changed it to black.

2.1 Use the New Slide button to create the next slide

◆

When you have completed the black slide described in Chapter 1, you are ready to create the next slide in your slide show. To get a new blank slide on the screen, do this—

✓ Go to the Formatting toolbar.

✓ Click on the New Slide button. A new slide with the Title and Text layout will appear on the screen. The Slide Layout Pane will be on the right side of the screen.

✓ Go to the Slide Layout Pane.

✓ Click on the Blank slide layout option. A new blank slide is now on the screen.

2.2 Put words or numbers in a box

◆

A box is designed so that you can type words or numbers into it. Once you put text into a box (or any of PowerPoint's other shapes), you can enhance the text in a number of ways using bold, italic, underlining, shadow, text alignment, color, different fonts, and changed font sizes.

PowerPoint has two types of boxes: the box made with the Rectangle button and the box made with the Text Box button. They have similar functions and some specialized capabilities which are summarized on the chart in section 2.7. This chapter uses the rectangle box. Chapter 3 covers the text box. For most applications, you can use either one, as you prefer.

A. Put a box on the new slide.

✓ Go to the Drawing toolbar.

✓ Click on the Rectangle button.

✓ Move your mouse pointer over the slide.

✓ Click to put the box on the slide.

The default size for the box (or other object) is one inch. The default fill color (the color inside the box) is a light blue. The default border is a ¾ point black line. All of these default choices can be changed. The steps for these changes are in sections C and E.

B. Add words and numbers in the box.

✓ Activate the box (click on it) so that its handles are showing.

✓ Then just start typing.

The default font size for text in a rectangle is 18 point. The default font color is black. The default font is Arial. These choices are what the software will use until you tell it to use something else. The steps for choosing something else are covered in section D.

You can use text of any length. If the text that you want to use is too long for the rectangle you have drawn, the text will extend beyond the borders of the rectangle.

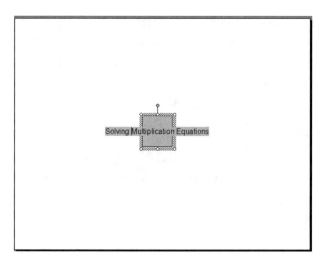

In this example, we have put the standard 1-inch box on the slide and then typed in the title for the slide shown at the beginning of this chapter. The title is too long for the box, so it extends beyond it.

When text is put in a rectangle, the text is centered (which is the default option for a rectangle). The text stays centered as you change the size of the box to accommodate it.

C. Resize the box to accommodate the text.

Using the middle handles on the box, you can stretch it across the entire slide. See section 9.3(D). In this in-stance, you can either stretch the box by dragging the middle handle on one side and then the middle handle on the other side, or you can stretch both sides of the rectangle at once by holding down the CTRL key and dragging one of the handles.

In the example below, the stretched-out box has been moved to the top of the slide where it will serve as the title. (To move the box, hold down the left mouse button and drag it into position. Be sure that the dotted border is showing; otherwise, it will not move.)

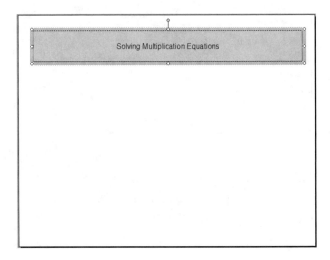

The stretched-out box also has been centered on the slide. You can do this by eye, or you can match up the center handles with the vertical Guide, which is discussed in section 2.3(B).

D. Use the dotted border to enhance the text.

PowerPoint uses the borders of its boxes and other objects to set up for making changes to the content of the box.

Before you put any text into a box, it has a simple line border displaying its handles. When you start to type text into a box, it displays a hatched border. This means it is ready to receive typed input. When you want to change the size, color, style, or other aspects of the text in a box (or the box itself), you need the dotted border.

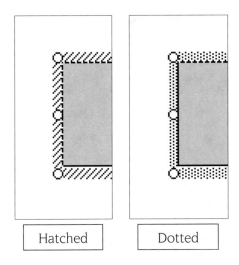

Hatched	Dotted

Some of the enhancements to the text in a box, for example, the font size, would typically be made when the
box is created. However, others, such as font color, might
not be made until the layout has been completed.

1. Activate the dotted border.

If the hatched border is showing, just move your mouse
pointer anywhere over the border (the four-point arrow mouse pointer shape will appear) and click. It will
change from hatched to dotted. The software tries to
anticipate what you are going to do, so the dotted border often will come up automatically.

2. Change the font size.

The default font size is 18 point. To change it, go to

the Formatting toolbar at the top of
the screen. Click on the button showing the large A, which is the Increase
Font Size button. Each time you click
on this button, the font size will increase. The button

next to it, with the small A, is the Decrease Font Size button.

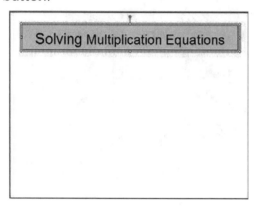

In this example, the font size has been increased to 44 point.

3.   Change the font.

The default font is Arial. To use a different font (or type style), go to the Formatting toolbar, at the far left, and click on the small down arrow next to the Font box. This will display the choices available. Click on any choice on the list, and the font will automatically change.

4.   Change the font color.

The default font color is black. To change the font color, go to the Drawing toolbar. The currently active color will be displayed in the small bar on the Font Color button. Click on the small down arrow next to the Font Color button. A small dialog box will appear displaying currently available colors. If none of these are what you want, click on the option "More Font Colors." This will display the entire spectrum of colors.

For the slide at the beginning of this chapter, the teacher has decided to use a white font color on a dark gray background. Because it is difficult to work with a white font color as the slide is being laid out, the teacher will leave the font color in black and change all the boxes to white at the end of the process.

5. Use emphasis (bold, italic, underline, shadow).

All of the normal word processing emphasis styles are available in Power-Point. To apply empha-sis, make sure the dotted border is active, go to the Formatting toolbar, which contains the buttons for Bold, Italic, Underline, and Shadow. Click on the button for the emphasis style you need. The text will change automatically.

6. Change placement (left, center, right).

The default placement for the text in a rectangle box is cen-tered. However, you can change the placement to flush left or flush right. With the dotted bor-der active, go to the Formatting toolbar, which con-tains the buttons for Align Left, Align Center, and Align Right. Click on one of the buttons. The text will change automatically.

E. Use the dotted border to enhance the box.

PowerPoint also uses the dotted borders of its boxes and other objects to set up for making changes to the box itself.

When you create a rectangle, it has a light blue fill and a black ¾ inch line border. Both of these features can be changed using the dotted border. If the box will be duplicated, these enhancements to the box would typically be made when the box is created because the duplicate will carry all of the style choices with it. However, these choices are affected by the background and the other design elements on the slide and might not be made until the layout has been completed.

1. Activate the dotted border.

If the hatched border is showing, just move your mouse pointer anywhere over the border (the four-point arrow mouse pointer shape will appear) and click. It will change from hatched to dotted.

2. Change the fill color.

 The *fill color* is the color within an object like a box or circle. The default fill color is light blue. To change the fill color, go to the Drawing toolbar. The currently active color will be displayed in the small bar on the Fill Color button. Click on the small down arrow next to the Fill Color button. A small dialog box will appear displaying currently available colors. If none of these are what you want, click on the option "More Fill Colors." This will display the entire spectrum of colors. Make sure the Standard tab is selected, and pick the color of your choice. Then click OK.

3. Change the line size.

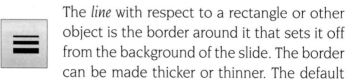 The *line* with respect to a rectangle or other object is the border around it that sets it off from the background of the slide. The border can be made thicker or thinner. The default line size is ¾ point. To change the line size to make it larger or smaller, go to the Drawing toolbar. Click on

the Line Style button shown here. A dialog box show-ing a range of line sizes will appear. Click on the size you want.

4. Change the line color.

The default line color is black. To change the line color, go to the Drawing toolbar. The currently active color  will be displayed in the small bar on the Line Color button. Click on the small down arrow next to the Line Color button. A small dialog box will appear displaying currently available colors. If none of these are what you want, click on the option "More Line Colors." This will display the entire spectrum of colors. Make sure the Standard tab is selected, and pick the color of your choice. Then click OK.

2.3 Work with several boxes

To complete the design of the slide shown at the begin-ning of this chapter, we will need to add more boxes. This section describes how to work with several boxes on a slide and to enhance the boxes.

A. Create a set of three boxes.

In the sample slide at the beginning of this chapter, the teacher has three formulas, and each formula is made up of three boxes. For example, the first formula is

| 3x | = | 120 |

1. Create the first box.

    ✓ Draw a box. Go to the Drawing toolbar, click on
    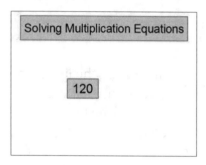
    the Rectangle button. Move your mouse pointer to the slide. The pointer shape will change to a cross. Hold down the left mouse button and drag to create the appropriate size for the box.

    ✓ Put the longest text in the box. This way, when you duplicate this box (to save work), the duplicate boxes will accommodate whatever text you need. In this case, the number 120 has more digits than any other text that will be put in a box. (When the box is active, you can type text into the box.)

    ✓ Pick the font and font size for the text. The easiest way to select the proper font size is to use the

    Increase Font Size button on the Formatting toolbar, which look like this. With the dotted border showing, click on this button until the size looks just right. If it looks too large, click the Decrease Font Size button right next to it. The font in the sample slide is Arial and the font size is 48 point.

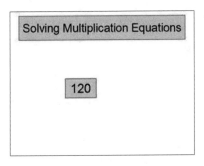

✓Get the box to the size and shape you need for the size of the text. Hold down the left mouse button and drag the handles on the box.

If it later turns out that you need a different font or font size, those changes are easy to make, and they are discussed in subsection 2.1(D).

2. Duplicate the box twice. (CTRL+D two times.)

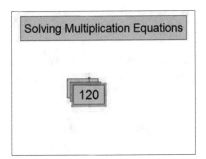

The two duplicates will appear just to the right and below the original.

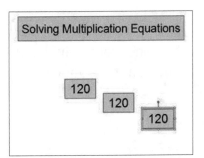

Move the duplicates apart. (Click on the box to activate it, hold down the mouse button, and drag.)

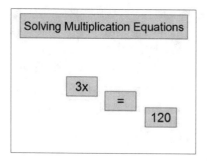

✓ Enter correct text into the first two boxes. (Highlight the text in the box by holding down the left mouse button and dragging across the text. Then type over it.)

B. Align the boxes.

When you have several boxes on the screen, you will want to be able to line them up in a way that makes the slide effective. PowerPoint provides two sets of tools for this work.

1. Display the Guides.

The Guides are dotted lines that can be displayed on the screen to help you line up boxes and other objects.

When the middle handles on the top and bottom borders of an object are aligned with the vertical Guide, the object is centered equidistant from the left and right margins.

When the middle handles of the left and right borders of an object are aligned with the horizontal Guide, the object is centered equidistant from the top and bottom margins.

To display the Guides, do this—

✓ Go to the Menu bar at the top of your screen.

✓ Click on the View button. A drop-down menu will appear.

✓ Click on the Grid and Guides option. A dialog box will appear; it looks like this.

✓ Check the box at the bottom that says "Display drawing guides on screen." Then click on the OK button. The guides will appear on the screen.

For the slide shown at the beginning of this chapter, the teacher is working on a white background because this makes the Guides easier to see on the screen. Although the final slide will have a dark gray background, this will be added at the end of the design process. If a dark gray background were used now, the Guides would be almost invisible.

In the example below, we have aligned the middle handles on the top and bottom borders of the title box with the vertical Guide, so the title box is now centered on the screen.

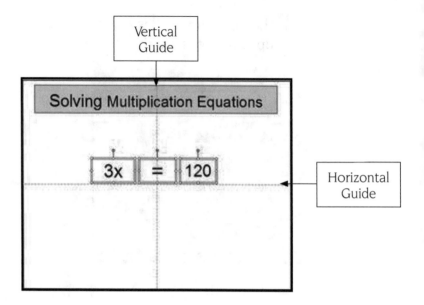

We have also lined up the three boxes containing the elements of the formula. One way to do this is—

    ✓ Move each box until its bottom border is resting on the horizontal Guide.

    ✓ Move the box containing the equal sign until the handles on its top and bottom borders are over the vertical Guide. It is now centered.

    ✓ Move the boxes to the left and right of the box containing the equal sign until they are evenly spaced.

In this illustration, all three boxes are active at the same time. Note that all three are displaying the dotted border. To do this, activate the first box, then hold down the SHIFT key on your keyboard and activate the second box. Do the same with the third box. You can now move all three together using the arrow key techniques discussed in section 1.6 B(2)(3).

2. Use the "Align" function.

Another way to line up boxes is to use the Drawing toolbar's align functions. To do this—

- ✓ Activate all three boxes by holding down the SHIFT key on your keyboard as you click on each box.

- ✓ Go to the Drawing toolbar.

- ✓ Click on the Draw button at the far left. A dialog box will appear.

- ✓ Click on the Align and Distribute option. A menu will appear.

- ✓ Click on the Align Top or Align Bottom option. The boxes are now even on either the top or bottom margin.

- ✓ With the boxes all still activated, move them so that they rest on the horizontal Guide and the middle box is centered on the vertical Guide.

3. Use the "Distribute" functions.

You can space the boxes evenly using the Distribute function, located on the same dialog box as the Align function. Once you place the box on the far right and the box on the far left where you want it, the Distribute Horizontally function will divide evenly the spacing of any boxes in between.

To do this—

- ✓ Activate all three boxes by holding down the SHIFT key on your keyboard as you click on each box.

- ✓ Go to the Drawing toolbar.

- ✓ Click on the Draw button at the far left. A dialog box will appear.

- ✓ Click on the Align and Distribute option. A menu will appear.

- ✓ Click on the Distribute Horizontally option. The boxes are now evenly spaced.

The Distribute Vertically function operates the same way. You place the top and bottom boxes where you want them, and the Distribute Vertically function will divide evenly the spaces of any boxes (or other objects) in between.

C. Use the No Fill option.

The default fill color for a rectangle box is a light blue. When you put the box on the screen, it comes with this color.

To put the numbers in the boxes directly on the background, delete the fill this way—

- ✓ Make sure the box is active (handles showing).

- ✓ Go to the Drawing Toolbar.

✓ Click on the small down arrow to the right of the Fill Color button, shown left. A dialog box will appear.

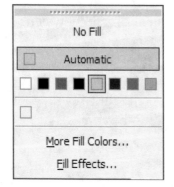

- ✓ Click on the No Fill option at the top of the box. The default fill color will disappear.

D. Use the No Line option to delete the border.

A rectangle box comes with a default border of a black line that is a ¾ point size. You can delete this line border so the text appears alone. To do this—

✓ Make sure the box is active.

✓ Go to the Drawing toolbar.

 ✓Click on the small down arrow to the right of the Line Color button, shown here. A small dialog box will appear, similar to the Fill Color dialog box.

✓Click on the No Line option at the top of the dialog box. The line border around the box will disappear.

2.4 Animate boxes (Wipe)

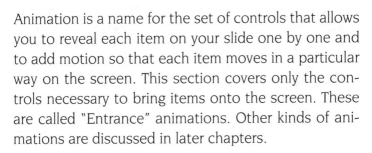

Animation is a name for the set of controls that allows you to reveal each item on your slide one by one and to add motion so that each item moves in a particular way on the screen. This section covers only the controls necessary to bring items onto the screen. These are called "Entrance" animations. Other kinds of animations are discussed in later chapters.

This section explains how to set up to add animation to box displays; how to animate the title and the individual boxes; then how to preview the animation and make changes, if necessary.

The fundamental purpose of animation is to keep your audience from reading ahead. You want them to concentrate on the point about which you are speaking. When you are using PowerPoint slides in a lecture or discussion, and you have a number of things on the slide, you can "animate" the slide so that each thing will appear at the time you want to talk about it. When your slide show is running, you can tap the space bar (or use a mouse click or remote control) to make the next object appear.

In the case of the sample slide in this chapter, the teacher would *animate the first set of boxes and then duplicate them* so that the next two equations animate in the exact same manner. The CTRL+D duplicate function carries all of the characteristics of the original box to the duplicate. This means that the teacher needs to do the animations only one time rather than for every box on the slide.

A. Set up to add animations.

Put the slide you want to animate on the screen if it is not there already. To do this, go to the Slides Pane on the left side of the screen. See illustration in section 1.3(A). Find the thumbnail of the slide and click on it. This will bring the slide to the screen.

1. Display the Custom Animation Pane.

The Custom Animation Pane is one of the displays in the Task Pane on the right side of the screen. To display it, click on the small down arrow next to the title on the Task Pane. A menu will appear. Click on the Custom Animation option.

If the Task Pane is not showing, see discussion in section 9.2(D)(1) to bring it up.

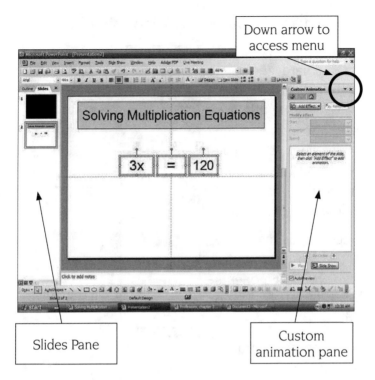

Down arrow to access menu

Slides Pane

Custom animation pane

2. Expand the Pane to full size.

Because the Custom Animation Pane contains a lot of detailed information, normally you will want to have it at full size. See discussion at section 9.2(D)(2) on how to expand the size of the pane.

3. Activate the AutoPreview function.

There should be a check mark in the AutoPreview box at the bottom of the Custom Animation Pane. This activates the preview function so you can see how the animation effects that you choose actually function on your slide. If the check mark is not there, click on the box to add it.

B. Animate the boxes: the Wipe animation.

First, decide whether to animate the title box at all. If there is *no animation*, the title box will appear with the slide when the slide appears. This can be a good option for the title of a slide.

Second, animate the three boxes containing the components of the formula. To do this—

1. Select the Entrance animation.

✓ Make sure the box that you want to animate is active.

✓ Go to the Custom Animation Pane, shown above.

✓ Click on the Add Effect button at the top of the pane. It will display a short menu with four options.

✓ Click on the Entrance option at the top. It will display another menu.

✓ Click on the Wipe option. If it is not displayed, click on the More Effects option at the bottom, which will display a complete list.

2. Decide how the animation should run.

Most animations give you options as to when the animation should start, in what direction it should move, and how fast it should appear on the screen. These options are displayed using the small down arrows next to the labeled boxes on the Custom Animation Pane.

✓ The **Start box** provides three options: On Click, With Previous, and After Previous. In this case, the teacher wants each box to come up as she clicks the slide show control, so the On Click option is chosen.

✓ The **Direction box** provides four options for the Wipe animation: From Bottom, From Left, From Right, and From Top. In this case, the teacher wants the text to be revealed in a motion from the left of the box, so the From Left option is chosen.

✓ The **Speed box** provides five options: Very Slow, Slow, Medium, Fast, and Very Fast. In this case, the teacher wants the text to appear quickly, and has chosen the Very Fast option. If these were more difficult equations, a teacher might choose the Fast speed instead.

Note in the illustration above that the software has numbered the first rectangle on the slide to be animated, and that rectangle now has its own listing on the Custom Animation Pane. Rectangle 1 contains the "3x." These separate listings allow you to animate each rectangle individually, to change the order in which the animations appear, and to remove the animations individually.

3. Animate the other two boxes in exactly the same way.

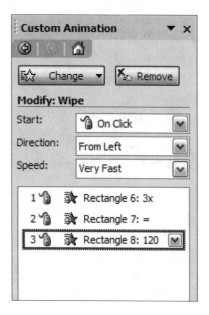

The Custom Animation Pane now looks like this. It has a listing for each of the three boxes and shows that rectangle #2 contains the = sign, and rectangle #3 contains the number 120.

Animations of text generally animate in one of these ways: Wipe, From Left; Wipe, From Top; Fade, Fast; or Appear.

C. Preview the animation.

Click on the Slide Show button at the bottom of the Custom Animation Pane. This will change the screen display so you are looking at the slide as it will appear when projected. Click on the space bar or click on the mouse to advance the animations and see how they will work. Changes in the animations can be made easily, and sometimes it is more efficient to wait until all of the animations are done to make changes.

D. Delete an animation.

To remove an animation, do this—

✓ Click on the listing for the animation to activate it.

✓ Click on the Remove button at the top of the Custom Animation Pane.

E. Change an animation.

To change an animation, for example, from Wipe, From Left to Fade, Fast, just to see how this will look, do this—

✓ Click on the listing of the animation you want to change. A blue border will appear around the listing indicating that it is active.

✓ Click on the Change button at the top of the Custom Animation pane to display the listing of available animations (note how this button changed from "Add Effect" to "Change" when you clicked on the listing and the blue border appeared).

✓ Select the Entrance effect of Fade and increase the speed from the Medium default to Fast.

✓ Click on the Slide Show button at the bottom of the Custom Animation pane to preview the new animation.

2.5 Finish up the layout of the slide

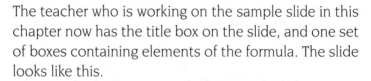

The teacher who is working on the sample slide in this chapter now has the title box on the slide, and one set of boxes containing elements of the formula. The slide looks like this.

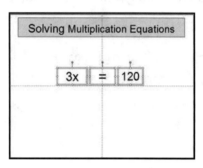

To finish up the work on this slide, the teacher would do this—

1. Position the first set of boxes.

Activate all three boxes containing the elements of the formula by holding down the SHIFT key as you click on each box. Use the arrow keys and Guides to move these boxes into the top of the screen and centered to where you want them. See section 1.6(B) for how to move objects with arrow keys.

2. Add and position the second set of boxes.

While they are still active, use CTRL+D to make a copy of these three boxes. Use the arrow keys and Guides to move these boxes down below the first three and into the location you want them.

3. Add and position the third set of boxes.

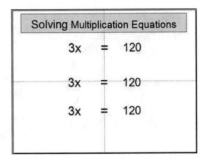

While this second set of three boxes is still active, use CTRL+D to make a copy of these, and then using the arrow keys and Guides, move these boxes down to the bottom of the screen into the location you want them.

4. Change the text in the duplicate boxes.

✓ Activate each box in turn.

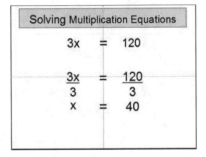

✓ Highlight the old text, and type in the new data. The old text will be replaced.

✓ Use an underline to create the fractions. To create the 3x over 3, place the cursor after the "x," hit Enter and type 3 again. Highlight the "3x" text. Go to the Formatting toolbar, click on the Underline button on the Formatting toolbar. Repeat to create the 120 over 3 portion of the formula.

5. Add the remaining design elements.

The teacher wants to put the principle "Divide by 3" on each side of the equation. To do this—

✓ Create one "Divide by 3" box. In this example, the font size is 40.

Solving Multiplication Equations

$$3x = 120$$

Divide by 3 | Divide by 3

$$\frac{3x}{3} = \frac{120}{3}$$

$$x = 40$$

Use inverse of multiplying by 3

✓ Animate the new box with the Entrance animation Appear, On Click. See section 2.4(B).

✓ Duplicate the box. (CTRL+D)

✓ Move the duplicates into place by dragging them so they line up under the title box. To move in small increments, hold down the ALT key while you drag the boxes.

The teacher also wants to display the principle that this method uses the inverse of multiplying by 3. To do this—

✓ Duplicate the title box at the top of the slide (CTRL+D). This duplicate will carry the same text size, font color, fill color, and animation as the original.

✓ Move the duplicate to the bottom of the slide.

✓ Type in the new text. (Highlight the existing text and type over it.)

✓ Resize the text to 40 point so that it matches the type size of the "Divide by 3" boxes. With the

dotted border showing, go to the Formatting toolbar, and click once on the Decrease Font Size button (the small A). The text in the box will be reduced from 44 point to 40 point. You can check this by looking in the Font Size box, also on the Formatting toolbar.

✓ Center the box on the slide by matching the middle handles on the top and bottom borders to the vertical Guide.

✓ Animate the box with an Entrance animation of Fade, On Click, Fast.

6. Add the background color for the slide.

In this case the teacher has decided to use a dark gray background. To add the gray background—

✓ Go to the Formatting toolbar.

✓ Click on the Background button. A dialog box will appear. See illustration in section 1.2(A)(2).

✓ Click on the More Colors option to get a full palette of colors, including the white through gray
to black on the bottom of the palette.

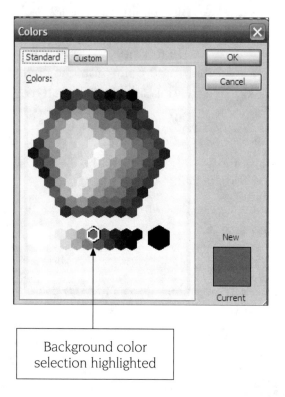

Background color
selection highlighted

✓ Click on the Apply
option.

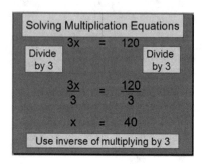

7. Change the font colors, as necessary.

The black lettering does not show up well against a dark gray background. To change the lettering to a white color in all the boxes at the same time, do this—

- ✓ Activate all of the boxes with lettering to be changed to white (title box at the top, formula boxes in the middle, explanatory box at the bottom) by clicking on the first box, then hold down the SHIFT key on your keyboard, and click on each of the other boxes in turn. (Another way to do this is to go to the Drawing toolbar and use the Select Multiple Objects button at the far right end of the toolbar and put check marks—by clicking—in the check boxes for all the objects except the two "Divide by 3" boxes.)

- ✓ Go to the Drawing Toolbar.

- ✓ Click on the small down arrow to the right of the Font Color button. A small dialog box will appear. An option for white font color is usually there. If not, click on the More Colors option to display the entire color palette.

- ✓ Click on the white color.

- ✓ Click on OK.

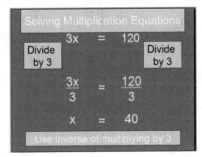

8. Add Shadow to the white text, if necessary.

 With the dotted border showing on the boxes where shadowing will be used, go to the Formatting toolbar, and click on the Shadow button. The shadow for white text is a very small black off-set for each letter which adds contrast.

9. Change the fill colors, as necessary.

The teacher making this slide has decided that the default fill color for the remaining boxes, which is a light blue, does not work well. Therefore, the two "Divide by 3" boxes will have a white fill within the box (to contrast with the black lettering); and the two boxes at the very top and bottom of the slide will have no fill at all, so the white lettering will appear on the dark gray background of the slide.

To change the fill color on the two "Divide by 3" boxes at the same time, do this—

✓ Activate both boxes.

✓ Go to the Drawing toolbar.

✓ Click on the small down arrow to the right of the Fill Color button. A small dialog box will appear. The option for a white fill color is displayed here.

✓ Click on the white option. The fill in both boxes will change to white.

To remove the fill on the two boxes at the top and bottom of the slide (so the background of the slide will show through), do this—

✓ Activate both boxes.

✓ Go to the Drawing Toolbar.

✓ Click on the small down arrow to the right of the Fill Color button. A small dialog box will appear.

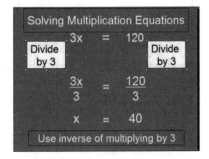

✓ Click on the No Fill option at the top. The default blue fill will disappear.

10. Delete (or change) borders on the boxes, as necessary.

PowerPoint puts a ¾ point black line border around rectangle boxes as a default. When the fill color is removed, the line borders remain. To remove the line borders, do this—

✓ Activate both boxes.

✓ Go to the Drawing toolbar.

✓ Click on the small arrow to the right of the Line Color button. A small dialog box will appear.

✓ Click on the No Line option at the very top of the box. The line borders will disappear.

11. Add the end-of-slide signal.

It is useful to have a small signal box on the slide that appears as a cue when you have reached the end of all the displays on the slide that have animations. This signal tells you that when you click on the mouse button (or press the space bar or the remote control) the next time, you will see the next slide on the screen.

Add the small signal box by creating a rectangle, reducing it in size until it is very small, and placing it in the lower right corner of the slide. (This is the same as creating the signal on the black slide as described in section 1.5.)

Use a light gray fill color for the small signal box so it shows but is a subtle presence.

Animate the little signal box with the Entrance animation of Appear, With Previous.

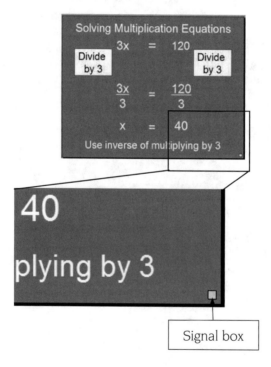

Signal box

12. Check the animations.

After all of the elements have been added to a slide, the last step is to check the animations to be sure that the slide "plays" correctly.

To do this—

- ✓ Go to the bottom of the Custom Animation Pane.

- ✓ Click on the Slide Show button. This will change your screen display so you will be looking at the slide as it will appear on a projection screen when you play your slide show in front of the class.

- ✓ Press the space bar (or click on the mouse button) to advance through the animations.

  To return to the Normal View: Right click with your mouse button. A menu will appear. Click on the End Show option.

13. Reorder the animations as necessary.

In this case, the animations for the two "Divide by 3" boxes are out of order. The teacher wants them to appear together after the first set of three formula boxes are on the screen. The software lists the animations in the order in which they are created, and in this case the "Divide by 3" boxes were created after all the formula boxes were already in place on the slide.

The PowerPoint display makes it easy to reorder the animations on your slide, no matter how many there are.

First, each object on the slide displays the number of its animation. In the illustration below, the enlargement on the left shows that the animation for the "Divide by 3" box on the left side of the slide is numbered 10.

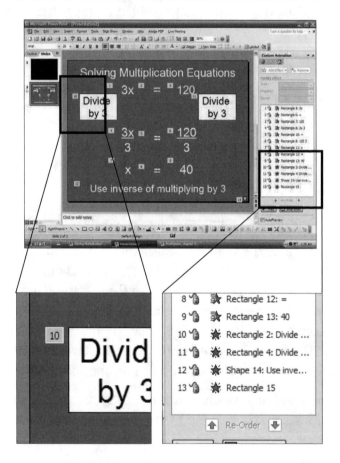

Second, each listing for an animation on the Custom Animation Pane is also numbered. In the illustration above, the enlargement on the right shows the listing numbered 10 that corresponds to the "Divide by 3" box on the left.

To move animation number 10 up in the order—

✓ Click on its name in the Custom Animation box so that a blue border appears. This animation is now activated.

✓ Click on the Re-Order Up Arrow at the bottom of the pane. Each click on this button moves the animation up one place in the order.

To move animation number 11 (the second "Divide by 3" box) up in the order, do the same thing.

To make animation number 11 appear at the same time as animation number 10, change the Start box from "On Click" to "With Previous."

2.6 Save your work

Go to the Standard toolbar at the top of the screen display.

 ✓Click on the Save button.

2.7 About rectangles and text boxes

Boxes can be made either with the Rectangle button on the Drawing toolbar or its near neighbor, the Text Box button, on the Drawing toolbar. Lists and outlines made with the special Title and Text layout on the Slide Layout Pane use text boxes.

When dealing with text on slides, some people find it faster to work with text boxes; others prefer rectangles. It usually makes no difference to the design, so long as you know how each of these objects works.

The features of these two objects are summarized in the table below. The shaded rows indicate differences; the white rows indicate similarities.

	Rectangle	Text Box
Shape	Can be drawn to any length and height.	Can be drawn to any length, but only to the height of one line of type until more type or spaces are added.
Fill	Comes with a standard blue fill that can be changed or deleted.	Comes with no fill. Fill can be added and changed.
Suitable for text	Yes.	Yes.
Text input	Text can be typed in any active rectangle.	Text can be typed in any active text box.
Text align	Default is centered, but can be changed.	Default is left justified, but can be changed.
Text length	As text length increases, rectangle size stays the same.	As text length increases, text box size increases.
Text size	As text size increases, rectangle size stays the same.	As text size increases, text box size increases.
Text effects	Bold, italic, underline, and font color are all available.	Bold, italic, underline, and font color are all available.
AutoFit	Does not keep text within the box.	Keeps text within the box.
Symbols	Available when hatched border is showing (after first letter typed in).	Available when box is drawn (hatched border automatic).

Shadow effects	Only standard Shadow available for text in the box; Shadow and 3-D available for box.	Standard Shadow and customized Shadow available for text in the box; no Shadow or 3-D available for box.
Line Border	Comes with a standard ¾ pt. black line border.	Comes with no line border. A line border can be added.
Input signal	When handles are showing, text can be entered. When text is entered, hatched border shows. When activated after text entered, dotted border shows.	When initially drawn, hatched border shows. When text is entered, hatched border shows. When activated after text is entered, hatched border shows.
Lines	Size and style can be changed. Color can be added.	Size and style can be changed. Color can be added.
Suitable for adding effect	Yes. Can surround words on a document for emphasis.	No. Can only display text typed into the text box.
Handles	Has four corner handles and four middle handles.	Has four corner handles and four middle handles.
Rotate	Has a rotate handle.	Has a rotate handle.
Connectors	Connector lines work.	Connector lines work.
Order	Bring forward, send back functions available.	Bring forward, send back functions available.
Bullets	Bullets and numbers can be added. Default is centered.	Bullets and numbers can be added. Default is left justified.

2.8 Sample slides from other academic subjects

◆

This slide from a physics lecture on wave fronts and rays uses two matching sets of three boxes to compare and contrast these two graphical representations of wave behavior.

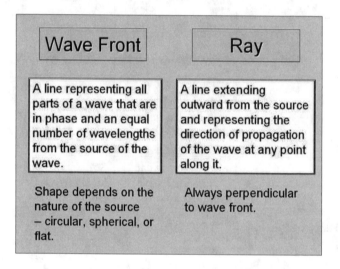

The title boxes have a colored fill to set them apart from the rest of the content of the slide; in this case, a light blue. The definitions are in Bevel boxes (Drawing toolbar, AutoShapes, Basic Shapes, Bevel) with a white fill. The descriptions of shape are in boxes with no fill.

Another type of slide built along the same lines uses circles (stretched into ovals), dotted border boxes, and colored fill boxes to differentiate concepts.

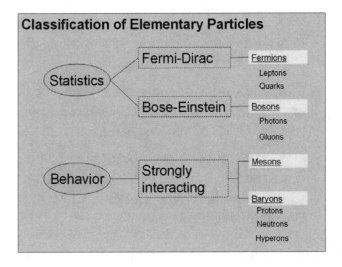

To construct this kind of slide, do this—

1. Draw the ovals.

   ✓ Draw a circle. (Go to the Drawing toolbar, click on the Circle button, move your mouse pointer to the area of the slide where you want the oval and click. This puts the circle on the slide.)

   ✓ Type in the longest word (in this case "statistics" has more letters) and increase the type size as necessary.

   ✓ Stretch the circle into an oval that will fit the longest word at the font size you want to use. (Drag the middle handle on either side outward to re-shape the circle to an oval.)

   ✓ Move the oval to the exact location you want.

   ✓ Decide on a fill color and apply it to the first oval. (Drawing toolbar, Fill Color button.)

   ✓ Decide on the animation and apply it to the first oval. (Custom Animation Pane.)

✓ Duplicate the first oval (CTRL+D).

✓ Replace the text in the second oval. (Highlight the old text and type over it.)

✓ Move the second oval into place. Using the down arrow key, move the second oval down to where you want it in the vertical plane.

✓ Line up the ovals. Select both ovals by holding down the Shift key and clicking on both, then go to the Drawing toolbar and click Draw, Align or Distribute, Align Left.

2. Draw the boxes.

✓ Draw the first box for the second column.

✓ Give the box a dash line border.

Go to the Drawing toolbar.

Click on the Line Style button.

Select 1½ pt. line.

Click on the Dash Style button right next to the Line Style button.

Select Dash (fourth one down).

✓ Duplicate the box twice (CTRL+D).

✓ Move the boxes to the general location you want.

✓ Retype the text.

✓ Resize the "Strongly" box as necessary.

Put your mouse pointer over the middle handle on the bottom border of the box.

Drag the handle down until the box enlarges to the size you want.

✓ Line up the boxes in the second column.

Select the "Fermi" and "Bose" boxes by holding down the Shift key and clicking on them.

Go to the Drawing toolbar and click on the Draw button.

Select Align or Distribute, Align Left.

Then hold down the Shift key and select the "Statistics" oval so that all three are selected.

Click on the Draw button.

Select Align or Distribute, Distribute Vertically. This will adjust the spacing for the "statistics" oval and its two subsidiary boxes.

Select the "Behavior" oval and "Strongly" box by holding down the Shift key.

Click on the Draw button.

Select Align or Distribute, Align Middle. This will line up the "Behavior" oval and its subsidiary box.

✓ Draw a box for the third column

✓ Follow the same procedure to duplicate the number necessary and line them up.

3. Use Connectors to draw the lines between the shapes on the slide.

✓ Go to the Drawing toolbar.

✓ Click on the AutoShapes button. A menu will appear.

✓ Click on the Connectors option. A dialog box will appear.

✓ Click on the Connector line you need (in this case, the Straight and Elbow connectors).

✓ Move your mouse pointer to the shape on the left. Small attachment points will appear. Hold down the mouse button and drag the connector line between the appropriate attachment point on each shape.

✓ Animate the Connectors and then the various boxes. Move each animated object Up or Down in the Custom Animation box to get the appropriate ordering.

Chapter 3
Outlines and Lists of Points to Accompany Lectures or Guide Discussions

---

Glacial Geology

1) What are "glacial periods?"

2) When have they occurred?

3) Why do they occur?

Glacial Geology

1) What are "glacial periods?"
   a. times of overall cooling of the earth's climate
   b. large portions of the earth's surface covered with thick glacial ice sheets

---

Glacial Geology

2) When have they occurred?
   a. Pleistocene epoch
   b. Paleozoic era
      Carboniferous and Permian periods
   c. Precambrian era
      Huronian time

Glacial Geology

3) Why do they occur?
   a. Agassiz: progressive cooling theory
   b. Croll: earth's heat balance changes as its orbit changes
   c. Milankovitch: earth's solar radiation changes as tilt changes

---

A basic outline or list of points, without any artistic effort at all, can increase the power of your teaching. An outline, either on one slide or a series of slides, helps get across the logic of your presentation and the facts that support your themes. It illustrates how one point is related to other points and makes the students feel comfortable because the structure of the presentation is apparent.

A good outline has a short title at the top and four to six evenly spaced one-line statements underneath the title. All of the points are directly related to the title. Each statement conveys only one thought. The text is stripped of all extraneous words. All that remains are the minimum words necessary to make the point. The oral presentation does the rest.

The skills outlined in this chapter will allow you to begin using polished lists right away.

Other sample slides for different academic subjects are set out at the end of the chapter. All of these slides are made in the same way.

3.1 Create an outline

You can construct a functional outline from start to finish by opening the Title and Text layout, adding a title, and adding outline points. Working on a good list of points helps hone your own thinking about your oral presentation.

A. Open the outline layout.

There are a number of ways to lay out an outline. PowerPoint has a preformatted layout called "Title and Text" that works well for outlines. It is sometimes also called the "Bullet List" layout. The easiest way to get this layout onto your slide is—

1. Go to the Formatting Toolbar.

2. Click on the New Slide button.

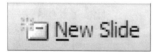 This button will display the Slide Layout Pane. The New Slide button usually displays the Title and Text layout as a default. If it does not, click on the outline layout on the Slide Layout Pane.

This layout has two **text boxes**—one for a title and one for the outline points. Text boxes are similar to the boxes created with the Rectangle button, covered in Chapter 2. However, they are designed specifically to contain text and have some different characteristics. These are summarized in section 2.7.

The screen will look like this.

B. Add a title.

1. Pick a title that summarizes a topic that you would cover in your lecture. In the example at the beginning of this chapter, the teacher has planned a lesson on glacial geology.

2. Move your mouse pointer anywhere inside the top box (where it says "Click to add title"). Click on the left

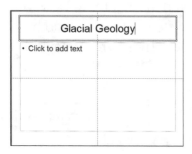

mouse button. The pointer is now an I-beam shape. See illustration in section 9.3(B)(2). Clicking inside a text box "activates" the box, and a hatched border appears around the edge of the box. See illustration in section 9.3(C).

3. Type the title in the title box. The text in a title box is centered automatically. The vertical Guide shows the center position. See discussion of Guides in section 2.3(B)(1).

4. Move your mouse pointer anywhere outside the title box. The pointer now changes back to the one-arrow shape. Click on the left mouse button. Now you can see how your slide looks thus far.

C. Add outline points.

1. Pick the points you would make about the topic that is contained in the title.

2. Move your mouse pointer anywhere in the lower box where it says "Click to add text." Click the left mouse button. The mouse pointer is an I-beam. A light circular outline point appears to the left of your pointer.

3. Start typing. PowerPoint is now working like a word processor. The text in an outline layout is aligned on the left margin.

4. Hit the ENTER key on your keyboard when you finish an outline point. PowerPoint will start the next outline point. If you make mistakes, just use the BACKSPACE key on your keyboard and type the text over again. The next section will show you how to edit the text.

5. Do not hit the ENTER key after creating the last outline point.

6. Click anywhere outside the text box to see your slide in finished form. The first draft of your slide is done.

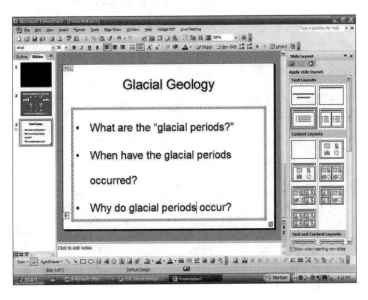

Always check your outline points to see if they can be further boiled down and, if possible, kept to only one line.

3.2 Edit an outline

◆

Editing text on slides is very similar to editing sentences in word processing work. If you use Microsoft Word, the commands in PowerPoint are the same. If you use another word processor, the commands are very similar. After you have typed text into a box on the slide, you can delete unnecessary words or entire outline points, add words or new outline points, reorder the outline points, and create subordinate points.

A. Delete unnecessary words.

1. Activate the outline box by clicking anywhere on the text in the box. Decide whether any of the words in the current outline points can be deleted.

2. Delete words in the outline box using any one of three convenient methods.

- ✓ *Backspace key*: Move the mouse pointer to a location at the end of the word to be deleted. Click to position the cursor there. Press the BACKSPACE key on the keyboard to delete each letter moving from right to left.

- ✓ *Delete key*: Move the mouse pointer to the beginning of the word to be deleted. Click to position the cursor there. Press the DELETE key on the keyboard to delete each letter moving from left to right.

- ✓ *Highlight+Delete key*: Highlight the words to be deleted by placing your mouse pointer at the beginning, holding down the left mouse button, and dragging the mouse to the end of the words.

Then release the mouse button. The text will be highlighted. Press the DELETE key. The highlighted text disappears.

B. Delete entire outline points.

1. With the text box containing the outline active, highlight all of the text of the outline point plus one space past the last letter.

2. Press the DELETE key on your keyboard. Even though you did not highlight the bullet point, when PowerPoint deletes all of the text associated with an outline point, it also deletes the bullet point.

C. Add words.

1. With the text box containing the outline active, place your mouse pointer on the line of text at the place where you want to add a word. Click your left mouse button. The cursor will be blinking at this point.

2. Type the word or words to be added.

D. Add new outline points.

1. Put the mouse pointer at the end of the outline point just prior to the new point.

2. Click to place the cursor at that point.

3. Press the ENTER key on the keyboard.

A new bullet point will appear, and you can type your text after it. In most situations, as you add outline points, PowerPoint will automatically reduce the type size if there is insufficient space on your slide for the new material. You can increase the type size by increasing the size of the outline box. See section 2.3.

E. Reorder outline points.

1. To move an outline point up in the order on the slide, click on the text to be moved (place your mouse pointer anywhere in the text and press the left mouse button), go to the Formatting Toolbar, and click on the Move Up button.

2. To move a outline point down in the order on the slide, click on the text to be moved, go to the Formatting Toolbar, and click on the Move Down button.

F. Create subordinate points.

1. Create a new outline point (as described in subsection D) containing the text for the subordinate point.

2. Go to the Formatting Toolbar.

3. Click on the Increase Indent button.

The shape of the outline will change and the new subordinate outline will be indented. Type your text as you would in making an outline point.

Alternatively, with the cursor at the beginning of the new outline point, press the TAB key on the keyboard to indent the outline point.

4. To make an existing outline point into a subordinate point, put the cursor immediately in front of the outline point, then click on the Increase Indent button.

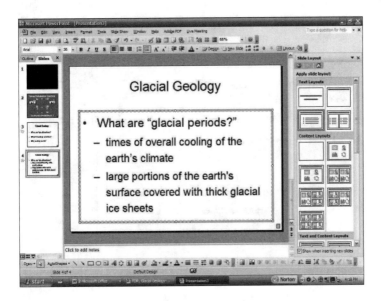

PowerPoint will automatically change the size and shape of the outline when a point is subordinated. The size of the type is also reduced.

5. To reverse a subordinate point (and send it back to the margin as a regular outline point), put the cursor 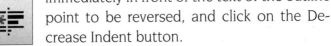 immediately in front of the text of the outline point to be reversed, and click on the De-crease Indent button.

Alternatively, with the cursor at the beginning of the new outline point, hold down the SHIFT key on the keyboard and press the TAB key on the keyboard for the same result.

6. To make a further subordinate point, create a new subordinate point and then click on the Increase In-dent button (as above). The point will be indented further and the style of the bullet point will change automatically.

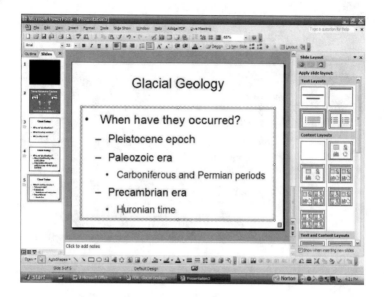

3.3 Enhance the outline text using the dotted border

◆

Nearly everything that you want to do to the text in an outline can be accomplished quickly using the dotted border.

When you are typing in text or editing text, the *hatched border* is showing around the outside margin of the box. When you want to change font size, add font or fill color, or use various kinds of emphasis, you need to have the *dotted border* showing. To change from one to the other, just put your mouse pointer over any portion of the border and click on it. The software will switch from one border to the other. See section 9.3(C)(3).

A. Change the size of the text.

The default font size for titles is 44 point. For outline points in the text box it is 32 point.

- ✓ With the dotted border showing—

- ✓ Go to the Formatting toolbar.

- ✓ Click on the Increase Font Size button or the Decrease Font Size button. All the text within the box will increase or decrease in size.

Consider these combinations for title and text sizes:

Title	Text
44 point	36 point
40 point	36 point
36 point	32 point
32 point	28 point

The size you have chosen will register in the small box to the right of the Font Box shown in subsection B below.

B. Change the font.

The default font is Arial, but PowerPoint has dozens of different font styles. To change the font, do this—

- ✓ With the dotted border showing—

- ✓ Go to the Formatting toolbar.

- ✓ Click on the small down arrow to the right of the Font box. A dialog box will appear displaying a long list of fonts.

Arial

✓ Click on the font that you want to use.

C. Change the color of the text.

The default color for text is black. In the sample slides shown at the beginning of this chapter, if the teacher used a dark blue background for the slide, it might enhance the slide design to use the same color for the text within the boxes (which have a light fill color). You can change the color of the text this way—

✓ With the dotted border showing—

✓ Go to the Drawing Toolbar.

✓ Click on the small down arrow to the right of the Font Color button. A dialog box with some color choices will appear.

✓ If the color you want is there, click on it; if not, click on the More Font Colors option to display an entire palette of colors.

D. Add emphasis to the text.

The PowerPoint features that add boldface, italics, underlining, or shadow all work the same way,

✓ With the dotted border showing—

✓ Go to the Formatting toolbar.

✓ Click on the button. The emphasis will be added to all of the text.

B *I* <u>U</u> **S**

To add emphasis to only part of the text within a box, highlight that text before clicking on the emphasis button.

E. Change the spacing between lines in the outline.

✓ With the dotted border showing—

✓ Go to the Formatting toolbar.

✓ Click on the Increase Paragraph Spacing or the Decrease Paragraph Spacing button. The spacing between all the lines in the box will increase or decrease.

F. Add fill color to the box.

✓ With the dotted border showing—

✓ Go to the Drawing toolbar.

✓ Click on the small down arrow to the right of the Font Color button. A small dialog box will appear. If the color you want is there, click on it; if not, click on More Fill Colors option.

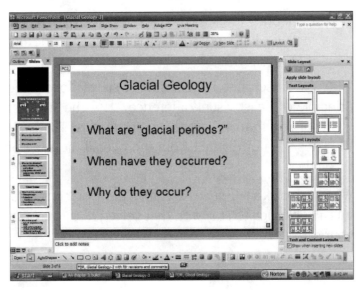

Delete the fill: With the dotted border showing, go to the Drawing Toolbar. Click on the down arrow next to the Fill Color button. A dialog box will appear. Click on the No Fill option at the top of the box. The fill color will disappear.

G. Put a line border around the box.

Text boxes do not have a border unless you add one. (The Rectangle boxes that were used in Chapter 2 have a black line border by default.) To add a border, do this—

- ✓ With the dotted border showing—

- ✓ Go to the Drawing Toolbar.

- ✓ Click on the Line Style button, which shows three solid lines. A dialog box will appear. It shows lines of various thicknesses.

- ✓ Click on the line size you want for the border.

- ✓ Click outside the box to see the line that is now in place. If it is not thick enough, choose another size.

When you use lines for classroom slides, follow the principle of "least visual difference." Use the smallest width of line that will get the point across. That way, the lines will not distract from the overall message of the slide.

When you pick a line style (size) for a particular purpose, it is a good idea to stay with that selection throughout your slides.

Color the line border: The default color for the line border is black. To make it a different color, go to the Drawing toolbar, click on the small down arrow next to the Line Color button. A dialog box will appear displaying several color choices. If the color you want is there, click on it; if not, click on the More Line Colors option to display a full palette of colors.

Delete the line border: With the dotted border showing, go to the Drawing Toolbar, click on the small down arrow next to the Line Color button. A dialog box will appear. Click on the No Line option. The border (which is a line) will disappear.

H. Resize and move the text boxes.

Any box on your slide can be made larger or smaller, taller or shorter, fatter or thinner. This capability helps with many design tasks. For example, sometimes as you juggle the words in your slide, you realize that you need to make the text box a little wider so your outline points can fit on one line, or a little taller so the spacing between your outline points can be increased for ease of reading.

1. Resize the box.

There are two ways to make a box bigger or smaller. You can resize by moving a single border or you can resize proportionally by moving all borders at once. The single border method is useful for making a box narrower, and the proportional method is useful for creating more space around a box on all sides.

To resize by moving a single border—

- ✓ Locate the single border handle you want to use. Single border handles are small circles in the middle of each border.

- ✓ Move the mouse pointer to a position over the handle. In order to drag a handle, the mouse pointer must be showing a two-arrow shape. You may have to move the mouse pointer back and forth a bit to get the two-arrow shape to appear.

- ✓ With the two-arrow mouse pointer over the handle, hold down the left mouse button and drag the handle in the direction you want the border to move. When you reach the right spot, release the mouse button.

To resize proportionally (all sides)—

- ✓ Locate the proportional handle you want to use. Proportional handles are small circles at the four corners of each text box. They make the box larger (if dragged outward) or smaller (if dragged inward) while maintaining the proportions of the box.

- ✓ Move the mouse pointer to a position over the handle. In order to drag these handles, the mouse pointer must be showing a two-arrow shape.

- ✓ With the two-arrow mouse pointer over the handle, hold down the left mouse button and drag the handle in the direction you want to change the overall size of the box. When you reach the right spot, release the mouse button.

2.   Move an entire box.

You can move the entire box up, down, and sideways to achieve better balance in the slide design.

✓ Move the mouse pointer over any part of any border that is not a handle. In order to move the entire box up, down, or sideways, the mouse pointer must be showing a four-arrow shape. You may have to move the mouse pointer back and forth a bit to get the four-arrow shape to appear.

✓ Hold the left mouse button down and drag the box in the direction you want it to move. When you reach the right spot, release the mouse button. For finer movement control, with the dotted border showing use the arrow keys or CTRL+arrow keys.

I.   Adjust the style of the bullet points.

The PowerPoint outline layout comes with circular black bullet points that are matched in style and size to the typeface you have chosen and that have a standard spacing between outline and text. You can change these to numbered points or lettered points, or you can change the color of the bullets. On occasion, you may want to use a list that has no bullet points at all.

To change from round bullet points to numbers, do this—

✓ Click on the text box to activate it.

✓ Change to the dotted border.

✓ Go to the Menu bar.

✓ Click on the Format button. A menu will appear.

✓ Click on the Bullets and Numbering option. A dialog box will appear.

✓ Click on the Numbered tab. The display will look like this.

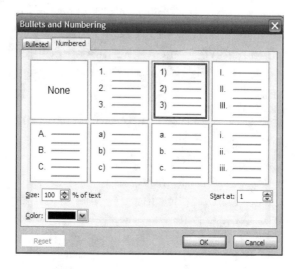

✓ Click on the number style you want.

✓ Click on the OK button at the bottom of the dialog box. The round bullet points will change to numbers.

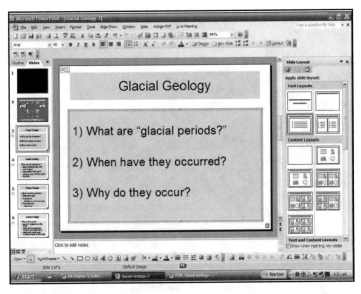

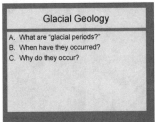

To change to letters, instead of numbers, click on a selection in the dialog box that shows letters.

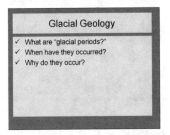

To change to check marks (or other bullet styles), click on the Bulleted tab at the top of the dialog box and choose the check mark style.

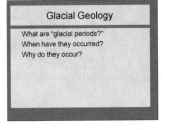

To change to no bullets, follow the directions above for changing to check marks and click on the option in the dialog box that says "None."

To *change the color* of bullets, click on the down arrow next to the small box labeled "Color" at the bottom left of the Bullets and Numbering dialog box and select an appropriate color.

To *change subpoints* from the default dashes to letters or numbers, click in front of the point to be lettered or numbered, go to the Menu Bar, click on the Format button, and select Bullets and Numbering. A dialog box will appear. Click on the letter or number style for that point. The dash will be replaced with a letter or number in the style you have chosen.

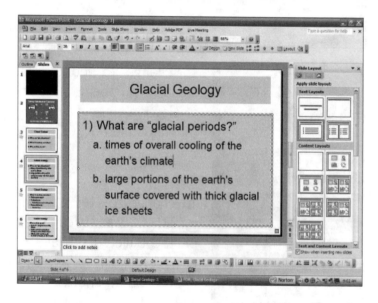

To *start a list with a number other than* 1 (for example, to explain point #2 on a second slide or when you want two successive slides regarding the same topic with continuing bullet numbers), go to the small box at the lower right corner of the dialog box and advance the "Start at" number to 2.

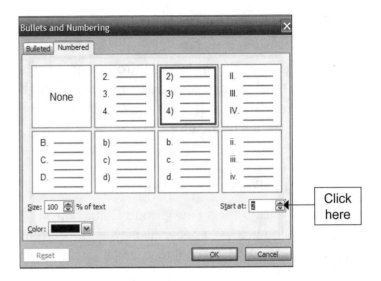

Click on the OK button at the bottom of the dialog box. The numbering will change to 2.

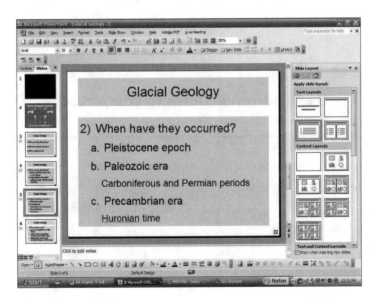

3.4 Add background color to the slide

In the illustrations shown in the introduction to this chapter, the teacher has added a dark blue background for the slide underneath the title box and the text box. This helps provide contrast for the text.

To do this—

- ✔ Go to the Formatting toolbar.

 ✔ Click on the Background Color button. A dialog box will appear displaying the current background color and a small down arrow next to it.

- ✔ Click on the small down arrow. A dialog box will appear with some color choices.

- ✔ If the color you want is on the dialog box, click on it; otherwise click on the More Colors option to display a full color palette.

3.5 Use a series of slides to complete the outline

In the slide series at the beginning of this chapter, the teacher has used four slides to complete the outline rather than trying to get all the information on one slide. To do this—

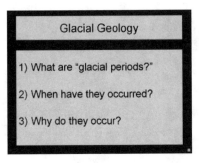

1. Make the first slide.

✓ Decide on all of the enhancements discussed in section 3.3, and add them to the slide.

✓ Decide on the background color discussed in section 3.4 and add it.

✓ Add the end-of-slide signal box in the lower right-hand corner as discussed in section 2.5(11).

2. Duplicate the first slide three times (CTRL+D).

These duplicates will form the basis for the rest of the slides in the series.

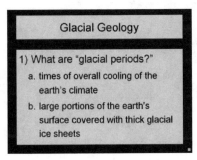

3. Make the second slide.

✓ Use the first duplicate slide.

✓ Delete outline points 2 and 3. (Highlight the text and use the Delete key on your keyboard.)

✓ Add the subordinate points that go with outline point 1. See section 3.2(F).

> **Glacial Geology**
>
> 2) When have they occurred?
> a. Pleistocene epoch
> b. Paleozoic era
>   Carboniferous and Permian periods
> c. Precambrian era
>   Huronian time

4. Make the third slide.

✓ Use the second duplicate slide.

✓ Delete outline points 2 and 3.

✓ Delete the text of outline point 1 and type in the text of outline point 2.

✓ Renumber this point so that it is number 2. See section 3.3(I).

✓ Add the subordinate points that go with outline point 2.

> **Glacial Geology**
>
> 3) Why do they occur?
> a. Agassiz: progressive cooling theory
> b. Croll: earth's heat balance changes as its orbit changes
> c. Milankovitch: earth's solar radiation changes as tilt changes

5. Make the fourth slide.

✓ Use the third duplicate slide.

✓ Delete outline points 2 and 3.

✓ Delete the text of outline point 1 and type in the text of outline point 3.

✓ Renumber the point so that it is number 3. See section 3.3(I).

✓ Add the subordinate points that go with outline point 3.

3.6 Animate an outline (Fade, Wipe)

The fundamental purpose of animation when dealing with outline point slides is to keep your audience from reading ahead. You want them to concentrate on the point about which you are speaking. The animation allows you to bring up one point at a time when you are using your slide show in the classroom.

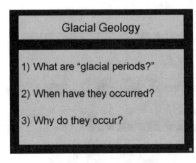

For example, if you were using the Glacial Geology slide illustrated here, you might want the title to appear with the slide, then the outline point "What are 'glacial periods?'" would follow. You would probably want the second point to appear separately just before you begin discussing this general topic, and then the third point to appear after the first two.

This section explains how to set up to add animation to outlines; how to animate the title and the individual outline points and subpoints; then how to preview the animation and make changes if necessary.

A. Set up to add animations.

1. Put your outline slide on the screen.

   ✓ Go to the Slides Pane on the left side of the screen. See illustration in section 1.3(A).

   ✓ Find the thumbnail of the first outline point slide and click on it. This will bring the slide to the screen.

2. Display the Custom Animation Pane.

✓ Go to the Task Pane on the right side of the screen.

✓ Click on the small down arrow next to the title on the Task Pane. See discussion in section 2.4(A)(1). A menu will appear.

✓ Click on the Custom Animation option. The Custom Animation Pane will appear.

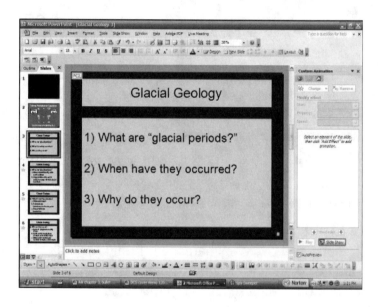

B. Animate the title: the Fade animation.

If you want the title to appear when the slide appears, then you need no animation. The purpose of animations is to control the way objects appear on the screen.

If you decide to have the title appear with some motion in order to add emphasis, you could use a Fade, With Previous, Fast animation. To do this—

1. Activate the title box by clicking on it.

2. Select the Entrance effect for the title.

An "Entrance effect" is the motion by which the text (or an object) arrives on the slide.

   ✓ Go to the Custom Animation Pane.

   ✓ Click on the button at the top that says "Add Effect." A menu will appear listing four types of effects. See illustration.

   ✓ Click on the Entrance option. Another menu will appear listing the available Entrance effects. The effects that are listed on this menu, and the order in which they are listed, can change. PowerPoint attempts to put within easy reach the effects you use the most. Click on "More Effects" at the bottom of the menu to see the rest of the list.

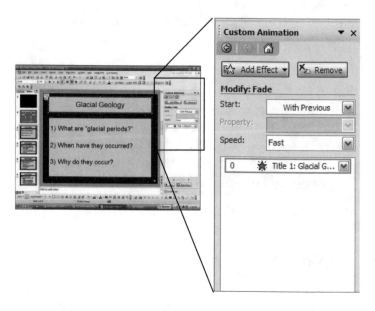

✓ Click on the Fade option. The automatic preview will show this action. This animation is now attached to the title box, and the screen display changes to reflect this.

✓ Go to the **Start box** at the top of the Custom Animation Pane. Click on the small down arrow. A short menu appears. Click on the With Previous option. This will start the Fade animation as the slide comes up.

✓ Go to the **Speed box** at the top of the Custom Animation Pane. Click on the small down arrow. A short menu appears. Click on the Fast option. This will move the title box to the screen fairly quickly.

To remove an animation: If, after looking at this animation of the title box, you decide it would be better just to have the title appear when the slide comes up, then remove this animation by clicking on the listing for the animation on the Custom Animation Pane. It will then be highlighted in blue. Click on the Remove button at the top of the Custom Animation Pane. The animation will be deleted.

Glacial Geology

1) What are "glacial periods?"

2) When have they occurred?

3) Why do they occur?

C. Animate the text in the text box: the Wipe animation.

An outline can be animated by activating the outline point box and applying the animation to the whole box, then making changes as necessary to the animation of particular parts of the outline box such as subpoints. In the kind of slide illustrated at the left, which has simple one-line points, the animation task is to make each of the individual points come up separately when the teacher clicks to advance from one point to the next.

1. Activate the outline point box.

2. Select the Entrance effect for the outline points.

   ✓ Go to the Custom Animation Pane.

   ✓ Click on the Add Effect button at the top. A short menu will appear listing the four principal categories of effects.

   ✓ Click on the Entrance option. Another menu will appear listing the first seven to nine types of Entrance effects. (There are fifty-two of these altogether. You can see them by clicking on the More Effects option.)

✓ Click on the Wipe option. Wipe is a good option for text because it brings the material to the screen in a motion that is somewhat like reading—either left to right or top to bottom. (If the Wipe option is not showing on the menu when it initially appears, click on the More Effects button and scroll down until you find it.)

✓ Go to the **Start box** at the top of the Custom Animation Pane. The default option is "On Click." This is the animation you want for your outline points.

✓ Go to the **Direction box** at the top of the Custom Animation Pane. Click on the small down arrow. A short menu appears. Click on the "From Left" option.

✓ Go to the **Speed box** at the top of the Custom Animation Pane. Click on the small down arrow. A short menu will appear. Click on the Fast or Very Fast option.

D. Adjust the animation of the fill in the text box.

When a text box *has no fill*, the animation you select for the box attaches only to the outline points within the box.

When a text box *has fill*, however, PowerPoint's default setting makes the animation attach to the fill as well as to the outline points within the box. There will be a separate listing called "Shape" in the Custom Animation Pane. This is the listing for the animation of the fill.

Normally you want the bullet text box with its fill to appear at the same time the slide comes on the screen. Your audience will realize you are about to put your points into this box. In order to remove the default animation of this box, click on the small double down arrow under the listing for the animation of the entire

Step 1   **Step 2**

box. This will display a separate listing for each of the outline points in the box. Click on the animation titled

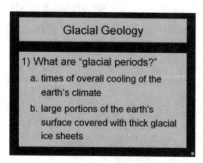

"Shape" so that it has a blue box around it. Click "Remove."

E.   Animate subordinate points so they come up separately.

The default animation is to bring subordinate points to the screen at the same time as the main outline point to which they are attached. However, it is usually better for a classroom presentation to bring up subordinate points separately. For example, in this case, the teacher would bring up the main point "What are 'glacial periods?'" and perhaps say a few sentences about this general topic. Then the teacher would bring up the first subpoint just before starting to talk about overall cooling; and would bring up the second subpoint just before starting to talk about the thick ice sheets. This keeps students focused on the point at hand and prevents them from being distracted by reading ahead on the slide.

To specify that each subordinate point is to come up separately, do this—

✓ Click on the small double down arrow under the listing for the animation of the entire box. This will display a separate listing for each of the outline points in the box. Notice that there are no numbers of symbols in the left-hand part of the

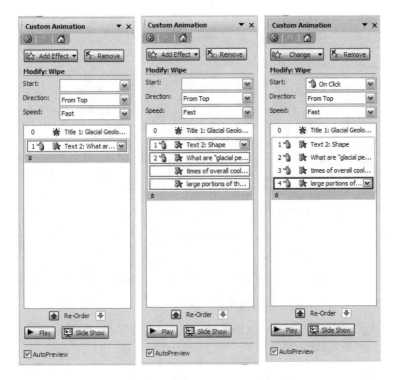

boxes representing the subordinate points. This means that they have no separate animation and will come up with the previous point.

✓ Click on the listing for the first subordinate point: "Times of overall cooling ..." The listing will be highlighted.

✓ Go to the **Start box**. Click on the On Click option. This will bring the first subordinate point to the screen separately.

✓ Click on the listing for the second subordinate point: "Large portions of ..." The listing will be highlighted.

✓ Go to the **Start box.** Click on the On Click option. This will bring the second subordinate point to the screen separately.

F. Preview the animation.

✓ Click on the Slide Show button at the bottom of the Custom Animation Pane and hit the space bar to advance the animations and see how they will work.

✓ Right click at the end. A small menu will appear.

✓ Click on the End Show option. This will take you back to the Normal View for working on your slides.

G. Make changes in the animation.

If you have followed the steps above, when you play the animation you can see that the three outline points appear in the correct order. No changes are needed.

The Custom Animation Pane anticipates two kinds of changes—animations in the wrong order and animations of the wrong type. To make changes, do this—

✓ Click on the listing of the animation you want to change to activate it. A blue border will appear around the listing indicating that it is active.

✓ To change the items that appear on the screen in the wrong order, go to the Re-Order buttons at the bottom of the pane. Click on the Up Arrow button. Each click moves the listing up one place. Click until the listing for the title is at the top.

✓ To change to a different animation, go to the Change button at the top of the pane. Click on it to display the listing of available animations. Click on the new animation.

✓ To change to a different Start, Direction, or Speed option, click on the small down arrow to the right of these boxes and select from the small menu the option that you want.

H. Delete an animation.

To remove an animation, do this—

✓ Click on the listing for the animation to activate it.

✓ Click on the Remove button at the top of the Custom Animation Pane.

3.7 Save your work

✓ Go to the Standard toolbar at the top of the screen.

✓ Click on the Save button.

3.8 Other examples of outline slides

PowerPoint provides an alternate format for outline slides. It has two text boxes and can be used for slides like this.

This slide outlines on the left the periods of Middle English Literature to be covered in the course, and on the right lists the types of literature that will be examined in each period.

Another type of outline slide uses three text boxes. A sample is shown. To set up this type of slide, do this—

✓ Go to the Slide Layout Pane.

✓ Select the Title and Text layout.

✓ Use your mouse pointer to decrease the width of the text box by using the middle handle and dragging to the left. See section 1.6(A).

✓ Duplicate the text box twice (CTRL+D).

✓ Resize the three boxes as necessary for the text they will contain.

✓ Align the tops of the boxes. (Hold Shift key and select all three boxes, then Drawing toolbar, Draw button, Align and Distribute option, Align Top selection.)

✓ Position the left and right boxes so that the margins are where you want them.

✓ Distribute the space between the boxes. (Hold Shift key and select all three boxes, then Drawing toolbar, Draw button, Align and Distribute option, Distribute Horizontally selection.)

Greek Word Roots

-anthrop-	human	• misanthrope, philanthropy
-chron-	time	• anachronism, chronic, chronicle
-dem-	people	• democracy, endemic
-morph-	form	• amorphous, metamorphic

A root is a part of a word that contains the core meaning of the word but cannot stand alone

✓ Type the text into the boxes.

In this example, the first two boxes are "no bullet point" boxes (see section 3.3(I)), and the third box has bullet points.

Stimuli for the Revolutionary War

- **Unfair taxation**

- **Lack of church choice**

- **Unfair treatment by**
  soldiers

Stimuli for the Revolutionary War

There were a number of different stimuli which precipitated the Revolutionary War. The Colonists were angered by the idea that the English Parliament could levy taxes without any representation for the Colonists. They were also angered that they had no right to establish their own churches as they saw fit. ...

An outline helps organize your thoughts before starting to write.

Another style for an outline box dispenses with the title and uses only the text boxes, perhaps with an explanatory box below.

To set up this format, do this—

    ✓ Go to the Slide Layout Pane.

    ✓ Click on the Title and 2-Column Text layout.

    ✓ Click on the title box to activate it.

    ✓ Press the DELETE key on your keyboard to delete the title box.

    ✓ Resize the remaining two text boxes to fill the available space and move them up the slide.

✓ Draw a text box for the bottom of the slide. (Go to the Drawing toolbar, click on the Text Box button, move the mouse pointer to the place on the slide where the text box should go, hold down the left mouse button, and drag to draw the box.)

In this case, the teacher has chosen a bullet point format for the text box on the left and removed the bullet from the first point "Stimuli for the Revolutionary War" by highlighting those words, going to Format, Bullets and Numbering, and selecting None, and clicking OK.

The text box on the right uses a no-bullet format which is accomplished by getting the dotted border, then Format, Bullets and Numbering, selecting None and OK.

One further step needs to be made to both of these boxes in order to remove the indenting on the second line of "Stimuli for the Revolutionary War"—

✓ Click View and select Ruler. Note the Ruler that has appeared in the top and left margin of the slide.

✓ Place the cursor in front of the word "Revolutionary" and click.

✓ Go to the top Ruler and note the margin tab and to its right the indent tab. Drag the indent tab to the left so that it is directly under the margin tab. This will move the entire second line to the left so that it lines up with the top line.

The text box on the left has a gray fill. The text box on the right has no fill.

Chapter 4
Illustrate Points with Photos, Maps, Charts, Graphs, and Drawings

Illustrations such as photos, maps, charts, graphs, and drawings are important educational tools. PowerPoint provides an easy way to enlarge them so that the entire class is looking at the same thing. In addition, you can label the illustration, focus on a particular part of it by cropping and enlarging, or point out certain features with arrows, circles, and boxes.

This chapter covers three aspects of slides that contain illustrations: first, working with the illustration itself by enlarging, rotating, and deleting it; second, enhancing the illustration by cropping, enlarging, labeling, and titling it; and third, animating the illustration to increase its educational impact.

Other sample slides for different academic subjects are set out at the end of this chapter. All of these slides are made in the same way.

4.1 Put an illustration on a slide ◆

The sample slide shown below is from a slide show for a physics course discussion about how the air flow over the top of a curved surface (in this case a rotor blade) creates lift. To make the point about the power of the lift, the instructor has chosen this photo of an ultralight aircraft which consists of little more than a seat for the pilot, a small engine, and set of rotor blades.

Illustrations put on slides are drawn from two sources—digital files already on hand (from a digital camera or scanned image) and paper copies that must be converted into digital form. This section deals with digital files. If you have a paper copy of an illustration, you need to scan it into digital format. You can use any home or office scanner for this purpose. Set your scanner to do images at 300 dpi for black and white and 150 to 300 dpi for color. Follow the directions that come with the scanner.

Illustrations used for educational slides are usually in a format known as JPEG (pronounced jay-peg). This format produces a relatively small file size and is the easiest for classroom work because the slides containing the illustrations come to the screen very quickly. Very large files load more slowly, so there is a period of waiting between the time you press the control to move to the next slide and the time the next slide appears on the screen.

A. Construct a blank slide to hold the illustration.

✓ Go to the Formatting toolbar.

✓ Click on the New Slide button. The Slide Layout Pane will appear on the panel at the right side of the screen.

✓ Click on the Blank slide layout option. See section 1.1 for more details and illustrations.

B. Import the illustration.

The process of getting the illustration onto the slide is called "importing" the illustration. This means that it is being brought from a file on your computer (or a CD, DVD, or other storage device, or the web) to the slide. PowerPoint treats all illustrations—photos, maps, drawings, and so on—as "pictures."

1. Display the Picture toolbar.

There is a special toolbar for working with "pictures." It looks like this.

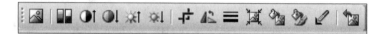

It should be at the bottom of your screen just to the right (and on the same level as) the Drawing toolbar. If it is not there, retrieve it this way—

✓ Go to the Menu bar at the top of the screen.

✓ Click on the View button. A menu will appear.

✓ Click on the Toolbars option. A dialog box will appear listing all the available toolbars. The ones currently displayed on your screen will have a check mark in front of them.

✓ Click on the listing for the Picture toolbar. The toolbar will appear on the screen.

✓ The toolbar may be floating in the middle of the screen. Put your mouse pointer over it, hold down the left mouse button, and drag the toolbar to its place to the right of the Drawing toolbar.

With the picture toolbar on the screen, you can create slides using any digital image. Remember, PowerPoint treats photos, maps, charts, graphs—any kind of illustration you have scanned—as a picture.

2. Use the Insert Picture button to put a photo on the blank slide.

✓ Go to the Picture Toolbar.

✓ Click on the Insert Picture button. A dialog box will appear. Its display depends on how your computer has been set up and what operating system you are using.

If you are using Windows XP, PowerPoint usually goes to the My Pictures folder as its default setting. However, you can navigate in the usual way to any folder where illustrations are stored. The illustration you want may be on the hard drive of your computer, on a CD, or even on a Web site.

✓ Click on the small down arrow to the right of the "Look in" box to open the file where the illustration is located. (The photos that are used in these illustrations are available at *www.nitastudent.com* in the folder labeled "Professors." To use these photos, open the folder, find the photo you want, click on it, use CTRL+C to copy the photo, then go to your slide, click on it, and use CTRL+V to paste the photo onto the slide), or

✓ Identify an illustration you want. Click on the thumbnail of the illustration (or file name for the file containing the illustration) to be put on the slide. A blue border will appear around the illustration, and its file name will be highlighted.

✓ Click on the Insert button in the lower-right corner of the dialog box. The illustration will appear on the slide.

The illustration should be centered in the middle of the slide.

Normally, PowerPoint will automatically resize the illustration to fit the slide. Some slide file formats cannot be processed automatically and may exceed the margins of the slide. In this case, you will have to resize the illustration manually. See subsection E for instructions in this regard.

C. Delete an illustration, if necessary.

If you change your mind about the illustration and want to substitute another one on the slide, you can delete the first illustration.

✓ Activate the illustration by clicking on it (the border and handles will be showing).

✓ Press the DELETE key on the keyboard.

D. Rotate the illustration, if necessary.

Occasionally someone has taken a photo with a digital camera that was turned 90 degrees to frame the photo in a particular way. In this case, the digital file will faithfully reproduce the camera angle and the photo will appear sideways when you import it. This can also happen if someone has scanned an illustration sideways. To turn the illustration right side up—

✓ Activate the illustration by clicking on it.

✓ Go to the Picture Toolbar.

✓ Click on the Rotate button. The illustration will turn 90 degrees to the left. If
more rotation is required, click on the
Rotate button again.

E. Center the illustration on the slide.

1. To position the photo so that the margin on the
top and bottom of the slide is the same—

✓ Activate the Guides. (Menu bar, View button,
Grid and Guides option, Display drawing guides
on screen, check box.) See section 2.3(B)(1).

✓ Move the mouse pointer over the photo. The
mouse pointer will turn to a four-arrow shape.

✓ Hold down the left mouse button. Drag the photo
to the center. Align the middle handles on the top
and bottom borders of the photo with the vertical Guide. Align the middle handles on the left
and right borders of the photo with the horizontal
Guide.

To make fine adjustments to center the document—

✓ Hold down the CTRL key on the keyboard.

✓ Press the ARROW key on the keyboard in the direction the photo should be moved.

2. To resize the photo so that it occupies as much of
the slide area as possible—

✓ Move the mouse pointer over a *top-corner* handle.
(Resizing with the middle handle will distort the
document.) The mouse pointer will turn to a two-
arrow shape.

✓ Hold down the CTRL key. (This will keep the document centered while you resize it.)

✓ Hold down the left mouse button. Drag the handle outward and away from the center of the photo. When you get to the size you want, release the mouse button.

F. Put a line border around the illustration.

Usually, it will be helpful to put a line border around the illustration. This makes it stand out from the slide. To do this—

✓ Activate the illustration.

✓ Go to the Drawing Toolbar.

✓ Click on the Line Style button, which shows three solid lines. A dialog box will appear. It shows lines of various thicknesses.

✓ Click on the line size you want for the border.

✓ Click outside the box to see the line that is now in place. If it is not thick enough, choose another size.

Color a line border: The default color for the line border is black. To make it a different color, go to the Drawing toolbar, click on the small down arrow next to the Line Color button. A dialog box wil appear displaying several color choices. If the color you want is there click on it; if not, click on the More Line Colors option to display a full palette of colors.

Delete a line border: With the border showing, go to the Drawing Toolbar, click on the small down arrow next to the Line Color button. A dialog box will appear. Click on the No Line option. The border (which is a line) will disappear.

G. Color the background of the slide.

✓ Go to the Formatting Toolbar.

✓ Click on the Background Color button. A dialog box will appear.

✓ If the background color you want is displayed there, click on it; if not, click on the More Colors option.

4.2 Crop and label illustrations

The meaning of an illustration may not be clear to the students without further enlargement or markings that help focus the students' attention on aspects relevant to particular issues being discussed. PowerPoint provides good tools for these purposes. You can crop, title, and label the illustration, and point out features with arrows, circles, or boxes.

A. Crop the illustration.

Cropping is a method for eliminating unnecessary portions of illustrations while maintaining the integrity of the remaining portion of the illustration. For example, if a photo includes two people, and only one person is relevant to the purpose of the slide, cropping can be used to excise the portion of the photo in which the other person appears. Cropping allows you to focus on a portion of the illustration and then enlarge it for easier viewing.

Cropping involves three steps—first, crop the illustration to isolate the part you need; second, resize the cropped portion of the illustration so that it is full-sized; and third, make fine adjustments to crop further as necessary. For example, in the slides shown above, the instructor has used a photo of the ultralight aircraft in the air, cropped it to focus on the aircraft, and then enlarged the cropped portion so that it fills the slide.

1. Use the Crop button to remove unnecessary material.

> ✓ Activate the illustration to be cropped. Move the mouse pointer over it and click once. The handles will appear.

> ✓ Go to the Picture Toolbar.

> ✓ Click on the Crop button. The handles will change in shape from round hollow circles to black lines.

> ✓ Put your mouse pointer over one of the *middle* handles as it is much easier to crop using these handles. The mouse pointer will change shape. As you move the mouse pointer toward the handle,

it will have the same shape as the icon on the Crop button. As you line the mouse pointer up with the handle, the mouse pointer will change to a T-shape. The top of the T will line up with the handle.

✓ Hold the mouse button down and "push" the handle in the direction you want to go. The margin of the illustration will move along with the mouse pointer. When you reach the point where you want the crop to end, let up on the mouse button.

If you crop too much: If you overcrop, you can take care of the mistake in one of two ways.

✓ Use the Crop tool to back out. The Crop tool will reverse itself if you drag the handle backwards, and will re-expose portions of the illustration that had been cropped off.

✓ Use the Undo tool. Go to the Standard Toolbar, and click on the Undo button one or more times. That will take you back to your previous move, and you can crop again.

When you are done: Click anywhere outside the illustration to turn off the Crop feature. The regular handles will reappear.

2.   Enlarge the cropped portion of the illustration.

Cropping usually reduces the size of the illustration to the point where it needs to be enlarged to make an effective slide. To enlarge it, do this—

✓ If the handles are not showing, activate the illustration by clicking on it.

✓ Hold the mouse pointer over a *corner* handle until the two-arrow shape appears.

✓ Drag the handle outward, to increase the size of the remaining portion of the illustration.

3. Crop and resize further, as necessary.

B. Title the illustration.

If you plan to explain particular parts of the illustration and to refer to those parts more than once, it is often useful to title the illustration so that its identification stays in the students' mind as long as the illustration is in view.

> Keep in mind that cropping is done with *middle* handles and resizing is done with *corner* handles.

To add a title—

Aerodynamic Controls for Flight

1. With the slide containing the illustration on the screen, and the illustration resized and moved to a location that will accommodate a title (see section 4.2)—

2. Draw a text box.

   ✓ Go to the Drawing Toolbar.

   ✓ Click on the Text Box button.

   ✓ Move the mouse pointer to the slide and click to place the text box on the slide.

   ✓ Move the mouse pointer over the handles on the box and drag to change the width of the box. See discussion in section 2.1(C).

3. Add the text of the title.

   ✓ Type the text of the title in the text box.

   ✓ Center the text within the text box. (With the dotted border showing, go to the Formatting Toolbar, click on the Center button.)

   ✓ Change the typeface and type size as necessary. Tahoma and Arial are good typefaces for classroom use. Titles are generally in a 40-point type size or higher. See discussion in section 3.3.

4. Put a border around the title box.

   ✓ Go to the Drawing Toolbar.

   ✓ Click on the Line Style button.

   ✓ Select a line size.

5. Resize the box as necessary.

6. Center the box on the slide.

Move the box until the top and bottom margins are equal and the side margins are also equal.

✓ Make sure the Guides are showing and center the box as explained in section 2.3(B).

✓ Hold down the CTRL key on the keyboard and press one of the Arrow keys on the keyboard.

7. Add color to the border, fill, and lettering in the box as necessary. See discussion in section 3.3.

Alternatively, if you know that the photo slide will have a title, you can use the Title Only layout on the Slide Layout Pane when you create the new slide. In that case, you would import the photo and size it to fit below the title box that is provided.

C. Label the content of the illustration.

Particular features of, or persons shown in, an illustration can be identified with labels so that the students will not get confused.

With the slide containing the illustration on the screen and the illustration resized and moved to a location that will accommodate one or more labels, do this—

1. Create a text box for the first label.

✓ Go to the Drawing Toolbar.

✓ Click on the Text Box button.

✓ Move the mouse pointer over the slide and click to put the text box on the slide. See section 2.2.

2. Put the text of the label in the box.

✓ Type in the text.

✓ Adjust the typeface and type size as necessary. (Dotted border, Formatting Toolbar, Increase/Decrease Font Size buttons.)

If there is a title on the slide, the labels should use the same typeface and a smaller type size than the title.

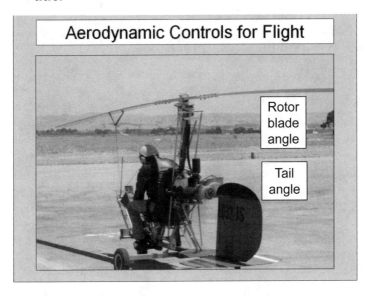

✓ Center the text within the text box. (Dotted border, Formatting Toolbar, Center button.)

3. Enhance the text box as necessary with color for the fill and lettering (in this example the fill is white and the lettering is black). See discussion in section 2.2(D).

4. Create a duplicate text box for the second label.

With the text box active, hold down the CTRL key on the keyboard and press the D key on the keyboard.

5. Replace the text of the original label with the text of the second label.

Highlight the text and type in the new text. The old text will be erased. Because this is a duplicate of the first box, it will have the same font, alignment, color, and border. However, if the text is longer, and if you want the size of both boxes to match, you may need to adjust the size of both boxes.

6. Position the labels on the slide.

✓ Move the duplicate box down on the slide to the approximate position you want.

To align the two labels on their left side—

✓ Activate both labels at the same time. (Activate one label by clicking on it; then hold down the SHIFT key on the keyboard and clicking on the second label to activate it.)

✓ Go to the Drawing Toolbar.

✓ Click on the Draw button. A menu will appear.

✓ Click on the Align or Distribute option. Another menu will appear.

✓ Click on the Align Left option. The left margins of the two labels will line up.

D. Point out features with arrows.

In some cases, there may be something about an illustration that is not immediately clear without a directional arrow indicating the precise location.

To add an arrow to the illustration, do this—

1. Draw the arrow.

    ✓ Go to the Drawing Toolbar.

    ✓ Click on the Arrow button.

    ✓ Move the mouse pointer to the approximate place on the slide where you want the back end of the arrow to start.

Pilot's tiller control

    ✓ Hold down the left mouse button and move the mouse toward the point at which the front end of the arrow should be. When you reach that point, release the mouse button. The arrow will appear on the slide.

2. Adjust the style of the arrow, if necessary.

    ✓ Activate the arrow.

    ✓ Go to the Drawing Toolbar.

✓ Click on the Arrow Style button. A drop-down menu will appear.

✓ Select the direction and style for each end of the arrow.

3. Change the thickness of the arrow, if necessary.

    ✓ Activate the arrow.

    ✓ Go to the Drawing Toolbar.

    ✓ Click on the Line Style button. A dialog box will appear.

    ✓ Click on the thickness that you want for the arrow. The arrow will be changed on the screen.

4. Change the length of the arrow, if necessary.

    ✓ With the arrow active and its handles showing at each end—

    ✓ Put the mouse pointer over the handle at the end where you want to lengthen or shorten the arrow. The mouse pointer will change to a two-arrow shape.

    ✓ Hold down the left mouse button. Drag the handle in the direction necessary to lengthen or shorten the arrow.

5. Change the color of the arrow, if necessary.

    ✓ Activate the arrow.

    ✓ Go to the Drawing Toolbar.

✓ Click on the small down arrow immediately to the right of the Line Color
button. A dialog box will appear.

✓ Select a color by clicking on the small box displaying the color or click on the More Colors button to see a palette with a wider choice.

In the slide illustration above, the arrow has been colored white so that it will contrast better with the background of the slide and the illustration.

4.3 Animate illustrations (Strips, Zoom, Wipe)

Illustration slides usually have considerable interest for
students and, while animation can add to illustration
slides under certain circumstances, in many cases no
animation at all is required. If you decide to use animation to make the oral presentation more effective, it is
a good idea to keep it to a minimum.

A. Set up to add animations.

1. Put your first illustration slide on the screen.

   ✓ Go to the Slides Pane on the left side of the
   screen. See section 1.3(A).

   ✓ Find the thumbnail of the first illustration slide
   and click on it. This will bring the slide to the
   screen.

2. Display the Custom Animation Pane.

   ✓ Go to the Task Pane on the right side of the
   screen.

✓ Click on the small down arrow next to the title on the Task Pane. A menu will appear.

✓ Click on the Custom Animation option. The Custom Animation Pane will appear. See illustration in section 2.4(A)(1).

B. Animate the title: the Strips animation.

If you want the title to appear when the slide appears, then you need *no animation*. The purpose of animations is to control the way objects appear on the screen.

If you decide to have the title with a decisive motion as the slide comes up to add emphasis, you could use a Strips, With Previous, Right Down, Fast animation. To do this—

1. Activate the title box by clicking on it.

2. Select the Entrance effect for the title.

   ✓ Go to the Custom Animation Pane.

   ✓ Click on the button at the top that says "Add Effect." A menu will appear listing four types of effects. See illustration in section 2.4(B).

   ✓ Click on the Entrance option. Another menu will appear listing the recently used Entrance effects. Click on "More Effects" at the bottom of the menu to see the rest of the list.

   ✓ Click on the Strips option. The automatic preview will show this action. This animation is now attached to the title box, and the screen display changes to reflect this.

✓ Go to the **Start box** at the top of the Custom Animation Pane. Click on the small down arrow. A short menu appears. Click on the With Previous option. This will start the Strips animation as the slide comes up. (The "Previous" in this case is the action of moving from one slide to the next.)

✓ Go to the **Direction box**. Click on the small down arrow. A short menu appears. Click on the Right Down option. This motion is in the general direction that people read.

✓ Go to the **Speed box** at the top of the Custom Animation Pane. Click on the small down arrow. A short menu appears. Click on the Fast option. This will move the title box to the screen fairly quickly but not too fast.

To *remove the animation*: If you decide not to animate the title after all, click on the listing for the title on the Custom Animation Pane. It will then be highlighted in blue. Click on the Remove button at the top of the Custom Animation Pane. The animation will be deleted.

C. Animate the illustration: the Zoom animation.

Often you will want the illustration to appear after the title has appeared on the screen. The Zoom animation is one good way to bring an illustration onto the screen. To add this animation, do this—

✓ Click on the illustration to activate it.

✓ Go to the Task Pane.

✓ Click on the Add Effect button. A menu will appear.

✓ Click on the Entrance option. Another menu will appear.

✓ Click on the Zoom option.

✓ Go to the **Start box**; click on the On Click option. This will bring your illustration to the screen when you give the signal by clicking on the mouse button, pressing the SPACE BAR or clicking on your remote.

✓ Go to the **Zoom box** (in other animations this is called the Direction box); click on the In Slightly option.

✓ Go to the **Speed box**; click on the Fast option.

Other animations that work well for photos are Fade, Fast; Faded Zoom, Fast; and Box Out, Fast.

D. Animate the label and arrow: the Wipe animation.

In this slide, you have a label identifying the joystick and an arrow pointing to it. Normally you would animate both the label and the arrow so they appear to the viewer to move in the same direction. The Wipe, On Click, From Left, Fast animation would be appropriate for the label and the Wipe, After Previous, From Left, Fast animation would work well for the arrow. Using the After Previous feature will bring the start of the arrow to the screen just as the label finishes rolling out.

To animate the label—

✓ Activate the label by clicking on it.

✓ Follow the same steps above. When you get to the list of Entrance effects, click on the Wipe option.

✓ In the **Start box**, click on the On Click option.

✓ In the **Direction box**, click on the From Left option.

✓ In the **Speed box**, click on the Fast option.

To animate the arrow—

✓ Activate the arrow by clicking on it.

✓ Follow the same steps above. When you get to the **Start box**, click on the After Previous option.

E. Play the animation to check it out.

Go to the Custom Animation Pane. Click on the Slide Show button at the bottom of the pane. The first item on the slide will come up. Click again to bring up subsequent items.

To go back to the Normal View: Click with your **right** mouse button. A menu will appear. Click on the End Show option.

4.4 Save your work

◆

Go to the Standard toolbar at the top of the screen. Click on the Save button.

4.5 Other slide designs for illustrations

◆

The most common designs for educational slides are shown in this section. They allow the educator to illustrate a point, make comparisons, and examine details.

A. Top and bottom text for an illustration.

An illustration in a scientific article can be scanned and put on a slide for easier explanation of the significance of the work. With all of the students looking at the illustration on the screen (rather than individually looking at a copy of the article at their seats), the instructor can be sure that the students are focused on the point being made through use of the illustration.

This kind of slide uses a title over the illustration and a short descriptive statement underneath the illustration. This is particularly useful to students because they can incorporate this illustration in their notes.

To do this—

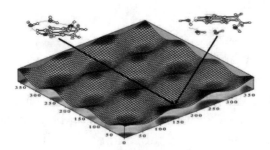

Tryptamine Monomer: Potential Energy Surface

Water bridges change the conformational preferences of biomolecules

✓ Use a Title Only slide layout.

✓ Put the text of the title in the title box.

✓ Duplicate the title box (CTRL+D).

✓ Move the duplicate box to the bottom of the slide.

✓ Put the bottom text in the duplicate box and reduce the size if necessary.

✓ Import the illustration.

✓ Resize the illustration as necessary to fit between the title box and bottom box.

B. Combine two or more illustrations.

Two illustrations, side by side or one above another, can help compare and contrast concepts or ideas.

To do this—

✓ Create a blank slide.

✓ Import the first photo. See section 4.1(B)(2).

✓ Crop and resize it to fit on half of the slide. See section 4.2(A) on cropping.

✓ Import the second photo.

✓ Crop and resize to match the first photo. (To re-size one photo to match another, right click on the first photo, a menu will appear, click on the Format Picture option, a dialog box will appear, click on the Size tab, and note the height of the first photo. Now go back to the second photo. Right click on it, a menu will appear, click on the Format Picture option, a dialog box will appear, click on the Size tab, and enter the same number in the height box. Click OK.)

✓ Align the tops of the two photos. (Activate both photos. Go to the Drawing toolbar, click on the Draw button, click on the Align or Distribute option, click on the Align Top option.)

C. Combine an illustration and a list of points.

If an illustration is to be used to explain several points, it may be useful to list the points with the illustration.

To do this—

✓ Create a blank slide.

✓ Import the illustration.

✓ Crop and resize the illustration as necessary. Move the illustration until it is centered on the slide.

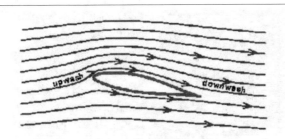

- The lift of a wing is equal to the change in momentum
- Momentum is the product of mass and velocity
- The lift of a wing is proportional to the amount of air diverted down times the downward velocity of that air
- For more lift the wing can either divert more air (mass) or increase its downward velocity
- Downward velocity behind the wing is called "downwash"

✓ Add a bullet point text box. (Go to the Slide Layout Pane, click on the Title and Text layout. See section 1.1(C). Then activate the Title box and delete it.)

✓ Resize the bullet point text box so that it fits underneath the illustration.

✓ Type in the text.

✓ Animate the points in the outline. See section 3.6(C).

This is the same type of slide with the bullet points arranged side-by-side with the illustration. It is constructed in the same way.

Microfluidics Devices

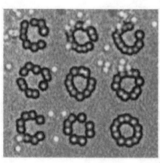

- Polystyrene spheres trapped in 3x3 array of optical vortices
- Created by 9 helical rings of light from a single Gaussian laser beam using a computer- generated hologram
- Entrain rapid flows from the surrounding fluid

D. Combine an illustration and a blowup.

To do this—

✓ Create a blank slide.

✓ Import the photo.

✓ Crop and resize the photo as necessary; move it to one side.

✓ Click on the Rectangle button and draw a box around the portion of the photo that you want to enlarge. Take out the Fill Color within the box so the underlying photo is visible. Increase the line thickness to at least 2¼ point so the box is more visible.

✓ Duplicate the slide. (Click on the thumbnail of the slide in the pane on the left side of the screen to activate it. Use CTRL+D to duplicate it.) This duplicate slide has the photo and the box on it.

✓ Crop the photo on the duplicate slide down to the borders of the box. This is the portion of the photo that will be enlarged. You can move the Crop control in very small increments if you hold down the ALT key while you are moving the mouse.

✓ Copy the cropped photo (CTRL+C) and paste it back on the original slide (CTRL+V). You are now finished with the duplicate slide, so you can delete it. (Activate the thumbnail, use the DELETE key on your keyboard.)

✓ Enlarge the cropped portion of the photo to the size that you need. (Drag a *corner* handle outward.)

✓ Move the cropped duplicate into position opposite the original photo.

✓ Draw lines connecting the box on the photo and the blowup. (Drawing toolbar, Line button, put the lines on the slide.)

✓ Position the lines to connect the box and the enlargement.

E. Use Clip Art and captures from Web sites.

Educational slides can be enhanced with Clip Art and material available on Web sites.

1. Clip Art.

Clip art consists of icons, stylized pictures, cartoons, symbols, signs, and other art material available in pre-packaged form. PowerPoint has its own collection of clip art, which you can access this way—

✓ Go to the Menu bar.

✓ Click on the Insert button. A menu will appear.

✓ Click on the Picture option. Another menu will appear.

✓ Click on the Clip Art option. This will display a dialog box from which you can select clip art.

The Microsoft Office Web site has a much larger inventory. To get there—

✓ Go to the Menu bar.

✓ Click on the Help button. A menu will appear.

✓ Click on Microsoft Office Online. PowerPoint will start your default Web browser, connect to the Internet, and take you to the Web site.

✓ Go to the panel on the left side of the screen under the listing "Home" and click on the "Clip Art and Media" option. A dialog box will appear.

It looks like this—

BROWSE CLIP ART AND MEDIA CATEGORIES

▪ Abstract	▪ Emotions	▪ Realistic
▪ Academic	▪ Fantasy	▪ Religion
▪ Agriculture	▪ Flags	▪ Sciences
▪ Animals	▪ Food	▪ Seasons
▪ Arts	▪ Government	▪ Signs
▪ Astrology	▪ Healthcare	▪ Sites
▪ Backgrounds	▪ Household	▪ Special Occasions
▪ Black & White	▪ Industry	▪ Sports
▪ Buildings	▪ Leisure	▪ Symbols
▪ Business	▪ Maps	▪ Technology
▪ Cartoons	▪ Nature	▪ Tools
▪ Character Collections	▪ Occupations	▪ Transportation
▪ Colorful	▪ Pastel	▪ Travel
▪ Communications	▪ People	▪ Weather
▪ Concepts	▪ Personal Appearance	▪ Web Elements
▪ Decorative Elements	▪ Plants	

✓ Click on a category. This will display a dialog box from which you can make a choice.

To search clip art across collections, do this—

✓ Go to the Drawing toolbar.

✓ Click on the Insert Clip Art button. The Clip Art Pane will appear at the right side of the screen.

✓ Enter a search term at the top of the pane, or go to the bottom of the pane and select the Clip Organizer button.

2. Captures from Web sites.

Many illustrations, charts, photos, drawings, and diagrams that you see on Web sites can be captured and put on a PowerPoint slide. To do this—

> - ✓ Put your mouse pointer over the illustration on the Web site.
>
> - ✓ **Right** click. A long menu will appear. It looks like the illustration to the right.
>
> - ✓ Click on the Copy option.
>
> - ✓ Go to your slide.
>
> - ✓ Put the mouse pointer over the slide.
>
> - ✓ **Right** click. A menu will appear.

The menu includes the following options:

Open Link
Open Link in New Window
Save Target As...
Download Later As...
Print Target

Show Picture
Save Picture As...
E-mail Picture...
Print Picture...
Go to My Pictures
Set as Background
Set as Desktop Item...

Set as Your Picture

Cut
Copy
Copy Shortcut
Paste

Add to Favorites...

View Original Image

Properties

- ✓ Click on the Paste option. The illustration will appear on your slide.

Alternatively, use the Save Picture As option on the menu to put the illustration into a folder on your computer from which you can retrieve it when you work on your slides.

Alternatively, if nothing else works, use the Print Screen button on your keyboard (usually located on the top row of keys at the right). When you press the Print Screen button, the software will capture an image of whatever is on the screen. The image will be stored on the Clipboard. You can locate it by displaying the Clipboard (Menu bar, Edit button, Office Clipboard option) or you can transfer it directly to a slide by clicking on the slide and then using the CTRL+V controls to paste the image on the slide. Crop the image down to whatever portion of the screen you wish to show.

Chapter 5
Document Slides for History, Literature, and Science Lectures

Document displays can be very helpful for a lecture focused on a particular passage in a literary piece, an event in history, or an explanation in an authoritative treatise. Not only does it add interest and help the visual learners to remember the point, it also teaches a vital skill—close and careful reading to discover key points of meaning and relationships.

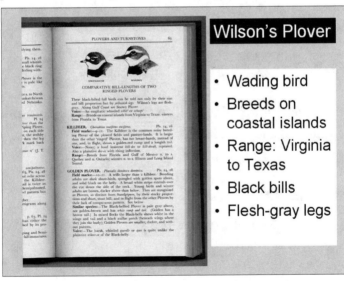

This chapter covers the basics: displaying a document on a slide; using blowups, boxes, circles, and callouts to focus on content; and applying basic animation.

5.1 Enlarge a document on a slide

The PowerPoint software treats a document like a picture: it uses the same buttons, functions, and options for both. For this reason, the process described in section 4.1 for putting an illustration on a slide is exactly the same for putting a document on a slide. Refer to that section for details. An abbreviated description is included in this section.

To display a document on a slide, you need to have the document in digital format; then you need to construct the blank slide to hold the document, import the document onto the slide, delete or rotate the document if necessary, put a line border around the document, resize and move the document, and add a background color to the slide.

If you have a paper copy of a document and you need to get it into digital format, you can use any home or office scanner to create the digital file

A. Construct a blank slide to hold the document.

Formatting Toolbar, New Slide button, Slide Layout Pane, Blank slide layout option. See section 2.1.

B. Import the document onto the slide.

Picture Toolbar, Insert Picture button, enter the location of the file containing the digital image of the document, click on the Insert button in the dialog box.

If the background on the slide is white, there will be no visible border around the document marking its outer edges, but the handles appear in the corners and in the middle of each edge.

If the document is too large for the slide: Move your mouse pointer over the document and click on the ***right*** mouse button. A menu will appear. Click on the Format Picture option. A dialog box will appear. Click on the Size tab at the top. Go to the Height box. Enter 7.3. Make sure the checkbox for Lock Aspect Ratio is checked. Click on OK. This will maximize the size of the image while still leaving a border at the top and bottom.

If you are importing a series of documents, make them all the same height, and all the images will be located on the same spot on each slide.

C. Delete a document, if necessary.

Activate the document by clicking on it, and press the DELETE key on the keyboard.

D. Rotate a document, if necessary.

Picture Toolbar, Rotate button.

Occasionally, documents are scanned sideways and, when imported, they will show up sideways on your slide. The Rotate button brings them upright.

E. Put a line border around the document.

Drawing Toolbar, Line Style button.

In some cases, in order to make the document look like a page (rather than just text on the screen), you need to put a visible border around it. For educational slides, it is usually a good idea to use the smallest line that will show up against the background you intend to use. This is usually the default line size (¾ point) or one of the next two sizes up. A heavy black line may make the document look somewhat artificial.

F. Resize and center the document.

1. Resize the document so that it fills most of the slide (from top to bottom).

   ✓ Put the mouse pointer over a corner handle.

   ✓ Drag a corner handle outward to increase size proportionally.

2. Position the document so that the margin on the top and bottom of the slide is the same.

   ✓ Activate the Guides. (Menu bar, View button, Grid and Guides option, checkbox for "Display drawing guides on screen.")

   ✓ Move the mouse pointer over the document. The mouse pointer will turn to a four-arrow shape.

   ✓ Hold down the ALT key and the left mouse button. Drag the document to the center so that the middle handles on the left and right borders of the document are aligned with the horizontal Guide.

G. Add a background color to the slide.

Formatting toolbar, Background button. See section 1.2(A)(B).

The background color might be a medium to light gray or similar color that causes the document to be the center of attention on the slide and does not distract the viewer.

5.2 Explanatory notes with a document

Most slide displays of documents need some explanation because the text of the document is too dense and small to be read easily at a distance. Adding explanatory notes to a document generally means using some form of box containing the necessary text. Sometimes it is a good idea to have more than one slide devoted to a document and to use different means to get across the essential points about a document. This is better than crowding a single slide with too much information.

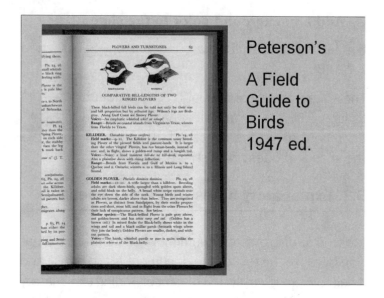

A. Explanatory boxes.

You can use a box to identify the document when it is first introduced.

1. Move the document to create space for the explanatory notes.

Normally the slide will display the document on the left and the explanatory material on the right. The document should be centered on the slide so the top and bottom margins are even.

2. Draw a text box or rectangle on the right side of the slide to contain the explanatory notes.

Drawing toolbar, Text Box button or Rectangle button. See section 2.2.

3. Type in the text.

4. Resize the box so that the text fits the space well.

B. Bullet point boxes.

Points to be made, drawing on the text of the document, can be summarized with a title and a series of bullet points.

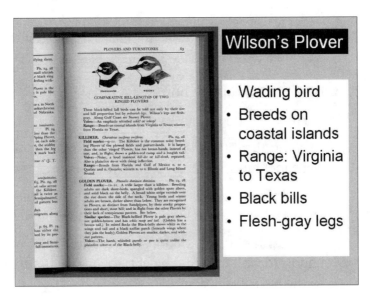

1. Set up the slide with the document at the left side.

2. Create the title box.

   ✓ Go to the Drawing toolbar.

   ✓ Click on the Text Box button.

   ✓ Move your mouse pointer to the place where you want to begin the box.

✓ Hold down the left mouse button and drag the box in the direction you want to go. When you get to the point where you want to end the box, release the left mouse button.

✓ Type in the text.

✓ Add the font color. (Drawing toolbar, Font Color button.) In the sample slide, the title is in white lettering.

✓ Add the fill color. (Drawing toolbar, Fill Color button.) In the sample slide, the fill is black.

3. Create the bullet point box.

✓ Go to the Slide Layout Pane.

✓ Click on the Title and Text layout. The software will superimpose that layout on your slide.

✓ Click on the Title box to activate it and press the DELETE key on your keyboard to get rid of it.

✓ Click on the Text box and use the left middle handle (drag it toward the right) to reduce its size to the available space.

✓ Type the text into the box.

✓ Adjust the size of the box to accommodate the text. (Dotted border, place mouse pointer over handle, and drag the handle.)

To maintain proportionality while changing the size of the box, hold down the SHIFT key on the keyboard while dragging the handle.

To extend the box from both ends (equally and at the same time), hold down the CTRL key while dragging the handle.

- ✓ Decide on the colors for fill and lettering. (Drawing toolbar, Fill Color button and Font Color button.)

- ✓ If you want to use a fill color, select one that will contrast well with the color of the lettering in the box.

To remove the fill from the box so that the identifying information will appear directly on the background of the slide:

- ✓ Go to the Drawing toolbar.

- ✓ Click on the small down arrow immediately to the right of the Fill Color button. A dialog box will appear.

- ✓ Click on the No Fill button. The color in the box will disappear.

C. Circles.

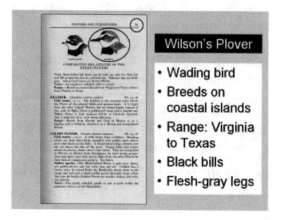

A circle marks a significant word or set of words in much the same way as a box, although it is less formal than the box. A circle mimics a natural action when a reader circles something on a document using a pen or pencil in order to focus attention on something that is important about the substance of the document.

A circle is added to a document in exactly the same way as a box, except you use the Oval button on the Drawing Toolbar instead of the Rectangle button. The Oval button actually produces a circle shape. The circle is modified to an oval shape using the handles.

5.3 Callouts: enlarged excerpts from documents
◆

Often the best way to make a point about a document is to highlight a phrase, sentence, or paragraph with a callout. This method involves copying a part of a document, enlarging it, and placing it on the slide ("calling it out" of the document) so that it is easier to see.

Callouts usually have an "anchor box" showing the

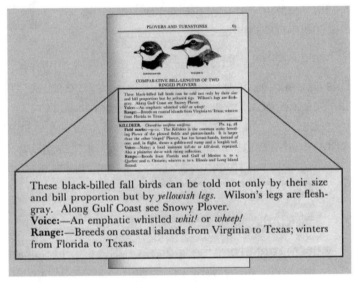

place within the document from which the excerpt comes. Callouts may also have lines connecting the callout to the anchor box.

This section explains how to make a "direct callout" which enlarges a portion of the text.

A. Set up the slide.

1. Get the document on the slide.

See section 5.1.

2. Move the document to the center of the slide.

B. Create the callout.

1. Put a box on the document around the material to be called out.

Drawing toolbar, Rectangle button.

This box serves as the visual "anchor" so the students can see the location from which the excerpt was drawn. Take out the Fill Color so you have a rectangle surrounding the portion of the photo you want to enlarge. Increase the line thickness to at least 2¼ point so the box is more visible.

2. Create the callout.

   ✓ Duplicate the slide. (Click on the thumbnail of the slide in the pane on the left side of the screen to activate it. Use CTRL+D to duplicate it.) This duplicate slide has the photo and the box on it.

   ✓ Crop the photo on the duplicate slide to the edges of the box exactly. You can move the Crop control in very small increments if you hold down the ALT key while you are moving the mouse.

✓ Copy the cropped photo (CTRL+C) and paste it back on the original slide (CTRL+V). You are now finished with the duplicate slide, so you can delete it. (Activate the thumbnail, use the DELETE key on your keyboard.)

✓ Enlarge the cropped portion of the photo to the size that you need. (Drag a corner handle outward.)

✓ Move the cropped duplicate into position, usually at the bottom of the full document.

3. Draw the lines connecting the anchor box to the callout.

✓ Go to the Drawing toolbar.

✓ Click on the Line button.

✓ Hold down the ALT key while dragging the line to get it to a length that fits.

✓ If the line does not quite connect as precisely as it should, zoom in on the area of the connection. 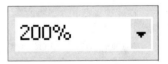 (Put your mouse pointer in the area to be the focus of the zoom, go to the Standard toolbar, click on the small down arrow next to the Zoom box, and select the amount of zoom.) Use the CTRL+ARROW key control to move the line to the precise spot where it should connect, or hold down the ALT key and drag the handle bar at each end of the line to the exact spot you want. Then use the Zoom box to go back to normal size.

C. Add colors, if useful.

1. Add background color to the slide. Formatting Toolbar, Background button.

2. Change the line color around the anchor box. (Drawing Toolbar, Line Color button.)

Like other shapes, the anchor box has a black line border around it when it is placed on the slide. If you are working with a document, you will want to change this color because a black line around black text is not effective. You might use an electric blue instead, found in the color palette on the second line down from the top, third color from the right.

5.4 Animate documents

This section explains ways to animate document slides. It is important that animation not distract the students from the facts that the document contains. Some document slides work well with no animation at all, and that option should always be considered.

The method used for applying animation effects to educational slides is the same regardless of the design of the slide.

A. Set up to add animations.

1. Put the document slide on the screen.

   ✓ Go to the Slides Pane on the left side of the screen.

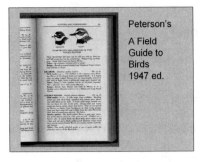

Peterson's

A Field Guide to Birds 1947 ed.

✓ Find the thumb-nail of the document slide and click on it. This will activate the document slide, and it will appear on the screen.

2. Display the Custom Animation Pane on the right side of the screen.

- ✓ Go to the Menu Bar.

- ✓ Click on the Slide Show button. A drop-down menu will appear.

- ✓ Click on the Custom Animation option. The Custom Animation Pane will appear.

B. Basic animation for the first slide (Box, Wipe).

The first slide has two objects on it—a page of an authoritative text, and a text box containing five lines of text identifying the author, title, and edition.

The animation for this slide is an example of basic animation for document slides.

In this case, assume that the instructor decided to show the page of the book first, followed by the identifying information. To do this—

- ✓ Click on the illustration to activate it.

- ✓ Go to the Custom Animation Pane.

- ✓ Click on the Add Effects button. A menu will appear.

✓ Click on the Entrance option. A list of Entrance animations will appear.

✓ Click on the animation to be used. In this case, the instructor decided to use Box, With Previous, In, Fast for the illustration.

✓ Click on the text box to activate it. Follow the same process. In this case the instructor decided to use Wipe, On Click, From Top, Fast for the text. This text has more than one line and is all in one box. The Wipe, From Top animation works well in that situation.

C. Coordinated animation with the next slide (Fade, Zoom, Wipe).

These two slides have the same basic layout. The size of the illustration on the left side of both slides is the same, and the size of the text box on the right side is also the same.

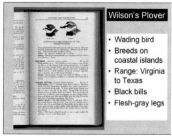

After introducing the source volume with the first slide, the instructor can visually replace that information with the details about the specific bird in the right-hand text box. Although the information remains on separate slides, to the viewer it will appear seamless.

To do this—

1. Take the text off the first slide with an Exit effect. (Fade)

  ✓ Activate the text box to be taken off the screen.

  ✓ Go to the Custom Animation Pane.

  ✓ Click on the Add Effect button at the top of the pane. A small menu appears.

  ✓ Click on Exit effect. A listing of Exit effects appears.

  ✓ Click on the Fade animation.

  ✓ Use the **Start box** to set the animation for On Click.

  ✓ Use the **Speed box** to set the animation for Fast. This will take the text box off the screen with one click.

Now the slide shows just the page of the document.

2. Make a seamless transition to the second slide by using *no animation* for the illustration of the page on the second slide.

This way, when the second slide comes to the screen, it looks just like the first slide with the text box removed because the page is in exactly the same place on both slides. Viewers will have the impression you are still on the same slide.

3. Put the title and text of the second slide on the screen with an Entrance effect.

- ✓ Click on the title box to activate it.

- ✓ Go to the Custom Animation Pane.

- ✓ Click on the Add Effects button. A menu will appear.

- ✓ Click on the Entrance option. A list of Entrance animations will appear.

- ✓ Click on the animation to be used. In this case, the instructor decided to use Zoom, With Previous, In, Fast. Using the Start option "With Previous" means that the animation of the title will start as soon as the slide comes up on the screen.

The text box has bullet points in it, and the instructor wants the bullet points to come up one at a time. To do this—

- ✓ Click on the text box to activate it.

- ✓ Go to the Custom Animation Pane.

- ✓ Click on the Add Effects button. A menu will appear.

- ✓ Click on the Entrance option. A list of Entrance animations will appear.

- ✓ Click on the animation to be used. In this case, the instructor decided to use the Wipe, From Left, On Click, Fast animation.

This text box has fill, so the box itself will be animated unless you remove the animation on this slide. See section 3.6(D).

D. Animate a callout.

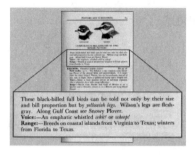

The callout slide typically has five objects on it: an underlying document, an anchor box, a callout, and two indicator lines connecting the anchor box and the callout. To animate the callout, do this—

✓ Animate the anchor box first with the Strips, On Click, Right Down, Fast animation. This will bring the anchor box to the screen with a motion that is similar to drawing a box around the text.

✓ Animate the indicator line on the left with the Wipe, From Top, On Click, Fast animation. This will cause the line to start at the box and run down the screen to the callout exactly when you decide the timing is right.

✓ Animate the indicator line on the right with the Wipe, With Previous, From Top, Fast animation. This will cause the second line to run at the same time as the first line.

✓ Animate the callout with the Wipe, After Previous, From Top, Fast animation. This will cause the callout box to unroll from the top just as the lines reach it.

E. Preview the effects.

✓ Go to the Custom Animation Pane on the right side of the screen.

✓ Click on the Slide Show button at the bottom of the pane. The slide will appear on the screen with the first animation.

✓ Click the mouse button (or use the SPACE BAR) to go through the animations.

✓ *Right* click at the end. A small menu will appear.

✓ Click on the End Show option. This will take you back to the Normal View.

F. Make changes as necessary.

If the preview shows that the animation should be changed, perhaps to a different Entrance effect, do this—

✓ Go back to the Custom Animation Pane.

✓ Click on the listing for the object that has the animation you want to change. The listing will be highlighted with a blue border. The "Add Effect" button at the top of the pane will now be a "Change" button.

✓ Click on the Change button at the top of the pane. A small menu will appear listing the four types of effects.

✓ Click on the option you need. A menu will appear listing the available effects.

✓ Click on your new choice.

✓ Click on the Start, Direction, and Speed attributes for the new Entrance effect, if necessary.

G. Delete an animation, if necessary.

Click on the listing for the particular animation on the Custom Animation Pane (a blue border will be showing), and click on the Remove button at the top of the pane.

5.5 Save your work

Standard toolbar, Save button.

5.6 More kinds of document slides

Most document slides are made using the techniques described in this chapter. Two kinds of documents—news articles and multipage documents—require additional steps.

A. News articles.

Some documents are displayed on slides just to illustrate that they exist. For example, a news article may be displayed for the purpose of explaining that there was a serious reaction in the press or that an event set out in the headline occurred in a particular way.

Greenspan Assesses Storms' Impact

By NELL HENDERSON
Washington Post Staff Writer

Federal Reserve Chairman Alan Greenspan said today that global economic growth will be slowed by the increase in energy prices caused by hurricanes Katrina and Rita.

"Although the global economic expansion appears to have been on a reasonably firm path through the summer months, the recent surge in energy prices will undoubtedly be a drag from now on," Greenspan said in his first public comments about the storms' economic effects.

The Fed chairman, speaking to Japanese executives in Tokyo, echoed the forecasts of many analysts, who have predicted that higher energy costs will force many consumers to curtail spending on other items and may cause some businesses to shelve expansion and hiring plans. A text of his remarks was made available in Washington.

Greenspan did not predict the magnitude of the drag on growth. But he did say that "the effect of the current surge in oil prices, though noticeable, is likely to prove significantly less consequential to economic growth and inflation than the surge in the 1970s." In that decade and in the early 1980s, high oil prices contributed to double-digit-percentage inflation and economic sluggishness — together labeled "stagflation."

Greenspan did not comment on the probable effects of higher energy prices on inflation or the Fed's plans to raise short-term interest rates enough to keep a lid on prices for non-energy items — both issues of intense interest to financial markets.

Greenspan said the storms hit at a time when "world oil markets had been subject to a degree of strain not experienced for a generation." Oil prices had been rising since 2002 as global economic growth caused energy demand to grow faster than supplies. The hurricanes slammed into the Gulf Coast in late August and September, shutting down and disabling oil rigs, refineries and pipelines. Energy prices soared 12 percent in September — the fastest rate since the government began collecting data in 1957 and contributing to the highest monthly consumer inflation rate in 25 years.

The balance of world energy supplies and demand, he said, "is so fragile that weather, not to mention individual acts of sabotage or local insurrection, could have a significant impact on economic growth."

A document that is a newspaper article may benefit from a white border around it. To do this—

✓ Create the blank slide.

✓ Import the news article.

✓ Draw a rectangle that perfectly covers the document by placing the cursor in the top left corner and clicking and dragging while holding down the ALT key for maximum control.

✓ Enlarge the rectangle proportionately to create a "frame" for the document by holding down the Shift and CTRL keys as you click and drag a corner handle.

✓ Change the fill color of the rectangle to white (or any other color you choose to make up the "frame").

✓ Put the rectangle behind the news article. (Go to the Drawing toolbar, click on the Draw button, click on the Order option, click on Send to Back.)

This is shown on Slide 1 below.

| Slide 1: Enlargement of the document with white rectangle | Slide 2: Anchor box showing area to be enlarged with a callout |

More commonly, some type of emphasis is used to point out what is important in the content of the news article.

Slide 2 above shows an anchor box added to the news article so that a callout can be used. This callout is made using the steps described in section 5.3.

This callout adds an underline for emphasis. To add the underline, do this—

1. Create the line.

   ✓ With the document on the slide, as shown in section 5.6(A)—

   ✓ Go to the Drawing Toolbar.

   ✓ Click on the Line button.

✓ Move your mouse pointer to the place where you want to begin the line.

✓ Hold down the left mouse button and drag the line in the direction you want to go. When you get to the point where you want to end the line, release the left mouse button.

If you hold down the SHIFT key on the keyboard while you are drawing the line, PowerPoint will know that you want a straight horizontal line or a straight vertical line, and the line will not go off kilter. If you hold down the SHIFT key and ALT key while you are drawing the line, you will be able to draw a straight, horizontal line in very small increments.

2. Adjust the width and color of the line, if necessary.

With the line active, and its handles showing at either end—

✓ To widen, go to the Drawing Toolbar and click on the Line Style button. The default line size will be highlighted. This is usually ¾ point. Click on the line size to be applied. The 2½ point size works well for underlining text.

✓ To color, go to the Drawing Toolbar and click on the small down arrow immediately after the Line Color button. A dialog box will appear. See illustration in section 3.3(G). The default color (black) will be highlighted. Click on the color to be applied.

Color helps make the underline technique effective. It is hard to see a black underline in a black and white document. A bright deep blue, such as the one on the second row, third from the right on the color palette, works well in this regard.

3. Adjust the length and position so that the line fits the words.

The line is an object, just like a photo or a text box. Its handles will respond to the same adjustments as other objects.

To adjust the length of the line—

- ✓ With the handles showing—

- ✓ Position the mouse pointer over one of the handles.

- ✓ Hold down the SHIFT key on the keyboard. (This tells the software that you want to draw a straight line in the same plane as the current line.)

- ✓ Use the left mouse button to drag the handle in the direction of the adjustment you need.

To adjust the position of the line—

- ✓ Activate the line so its handles are showing.

- ✓ Hold down the CTRL key on the keyboard and press the directional ARROW key on the keyboard (Up, Down, Right, Left). This will move the line in very small increments.

4. Animate the line.

Wipe, On Click, From Left, Fast.

B. Multipage documents.

Assume that you have a two-page document. You want to make several points about the content of the first page of the document, then display some of its important text from the second page and focus on one important section of that page. The easiest way to do this is to use two slides linked by their animation so they appear to be the same slide.

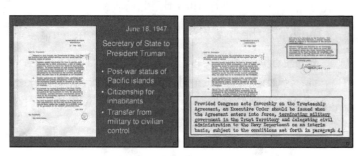

The first slide displays the document with boxes showing its date, the fact that it went from the Secretary of State to President Truman, and the principal points. It is constructed using the method described in section 5.2.

The next slide displays the second page of the document with a callout from its text and certain words emphasized with an underline. It is constructed using the method described in section 5.3.

It is imperative that the first page be in exactly the same position on both slides so that the transition from one to the other is seamless. To accomplish this, create the first slide with the first page of the document sized and positioned as shown on the previous page. Duplicate the slide by clicking on the thumbnail in the Slide Pane on the left so that it has a blue border, then CTRL+D.

Basic animation for the first slide (Box, Fade, Wipe).

The first slide has five objects on it—the first page of a two-page document, two labels (indicating the date and author/recipient), a text box containing three bullet points, and signal box.

The animation for this slide is an example of basic animation for document slides.

1. Bring each object to the screen with an Entrance animation.

In this case, assume that the instructor decided to show the document first, followed by the date label and the author/recipient label, and then to put each bullet point on the screen one at a time as the discussion about the document progressed.

To do this—

   ✓ Click on the object to activate it.

   ✓ Go to the Custom Animation Pane.

   ✓ Click on the Add Effects button. A menu will appear.

   ✓ Click on the Entrance option. A list of Entrance animations will appear.

   ✓ Click on the animation to be used. In this case, the instructor decided to use—

      Box, With Previous, In, Fast for the page so that when you come to this slide, the animation occurs at once.

      Fade, On Click, Fast for each of the labels.

      Wipe, On Click, From Top, Fast for each of the bullet points.

      Appear, After Previous for the signal box.

✓ Set the bullet points to appear one-by-one. Click on the small down arrow just below the listing for the animation. This displays the individual listings for each point. Make sure each one has an "On Click" icon in front of it. If it does not, go back to the **Start box** and add it.

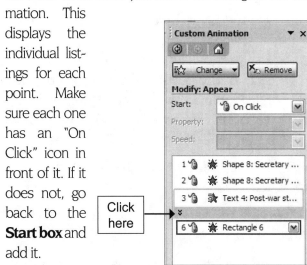

2. Take objects off the slide with an Exit effect. (Fade)

To move seamlessly from the first slide (which displays only the first page of the document) to the second slide (which displays both the first and second pages of the document), you need to take the labels and text box off the first slide after you have used them to discuss the first page. This is done with an Exit effect.

✓ Activate all four objects to be taken off the screen (the three boxes and the small signal box at the bottom right corner) by holding down the SHIFT key as you click on each one.

✓ Go to the Custom Animation Pane.

✓ Click on the Add Effect button at the top of the pane. A small menu appears.

✓ Click on Exit effect. A listing of Exit effects appears.

✓ Use the Fade, Fast animation for each of the boxes.

✓ Use the **Start box** to set the first animation for On Click, and the remaining animations set for With Previous (you may need to expand the contents of the bullets by clicking on the down facing double arrow and change each bullet point to "With Previous"). This will take all four objects off the screen with one click.

Now the first slide shows just the first page of the document.

Advanced animation for the second slide. (Motion Path)

The second slide has both pages of the document, with the second page stacked below the first page. Using the Motion Path animation feature, you can make the second page slide out from behind the first page and then display an enlargement of material excerpted from the second page.

1. Stack the second page on top of the first.

✓ Import the second page.

✓ Make the second page the exact same height as the first using the Format Picture dialog box. See section 4.5(B).

✓ Move the second page until it is exactly over the first page using the Align function. (Start with the second page to the right of and below the first page—move it there if it isn't already there). Then activate both pages by holding down the SHIFT key as you click on each, go to the Drawing toolbar, click on the Draw button, click on the Align or Distribute option, use Align Left, then repeat and use Align Top.

In the end, the second page will wind up under the first page, but for now it is easier to work with when it is on top.

2. Animate the second page with the Appear, With Previous settings. See section 2.4.

This will put both pages on the screen when the second slide comes up. At its beginning, the second slide will look just like the first one (because the second page will be hidden underneath the first page) and the viewer will be unaware that you have moved to a new slide.

3. Construct the callout of material from the second page.

Put a box around the callout, duplicate the slide, and crop the callout from the duplicate. Then resize and move the callout to the appropriate location on the slide. See section 4.5(D).

4. Animate the callout with the Faded Zoom, On Click, Fast settings.

See section 2.4.

5. Put an underline on the callout.

See section 5.6(A)(1).

6. Animate the underline with the Fade, On Click, Fast settings.

In this example, the important words occur on two lines, therefore the underlining is in two parts. Use the After Previous setting for the animation of the second part of the line so it will start up right after the preceding line is displayed.

7. Bring the anchor box (the rectangle surrounding the key text) onto the screen.

One option with regard to the rectangle is to group this anchor box with the page so they will move together.

- ✓ Activate both the anchor box and the page at the same time.
- ✓ Go to the Drawing toolbar.
- ✓ Click on the Draw button. A menu will appear.
- ✓ Click on the Group option at the top.

The Group feature glues the two objects together so that they work as a single unit.

Another option would be to have the second page slide out unvarnished and then have the rectangle appear on the screen to surround the key text. To do this—

- ✓ Draw the rectangle before moving the second page behind the first so that it is the exact size you want. Remove the fill, thicken the line, and color the line electric blue.
- ✓ Move the box out to the right using the right arrow key to approximately where you think it should be.

✓ Animate the box with a Strips, After Previous, Right Down, Fast Entrance effect. Put it in order right after the motion path of the second page as shown in 8 just below.

✓ Click on Slide Show to run the animations and see if the box is exactly in the right place or needs to be moved a bit right or left. By trial and error, place the rectangle in the exact location.

8.   Use the Motion Path animation to slide the second page to the right until it is all visible and does not overlap with the first page.

✓ Activate the second page.

✓ Go to the Custom Animation Pane.

✓ Click on the Add Effect button. A menu will appear.

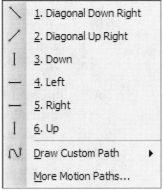

✓ Click on the Motion Path option. A dialog box will appear showing the motion options. It looks like this.

✓ Click on the Right option. A Motion Path arrow appears over the page, centered at its midpoint. This Motion Path arrow moves the page from left to right and governs how far the page moves.

The motion path arrow has a green end on the left and a red end on the right. The red arrow point has a small line in front of it. This is where the motion will stop. Your document will be centered at this point when the animation is completed.

✓ Adjust the length of the motion path arrow.

The default arrow will not move a document page far enough to the right. Therefore, you need to extend it. Put your mouse pointer over the red arrow point at the right end, hold down the SHIFT key (to keep it perfectly horizontal) and drag it to the right to make the arrow longer. This will move the page farther.

Be careful not to move the arrow itself. Leave it centered at the green end at the left. If you move the arrow by mistake, use the Undo button on the Standard toolbar to put it back in its original position.

Your mouse pointer should be a slanted two-headed arrow shape when it drags the red end to extend the length of the arrow toward the right.

If, when you run the animation, the second page does not move far enough to the right, extend the red arrow further to the right. Similarly, if page 2 goes too far to the right, back it up with the same arrow.

9. Use the Order feature to put the second page below the first page.

✓ Activate the second page so its handles are showing.

✓ Go to the Drawing toolbar.

✓ Click on the Draw button. A menu will appear.

✓ Click on the Order option. Another menu will appear.

✓ Click on the Send to Back option. This will put the second page underneath the first page.

10. Change the order of the animations.

You want the second page to slide out from below the first page and then have the callout appear after the second page has appeared from behind the first page. To do this—

✓ Go to the Custom Animation Pane.

✓ Highlight the animation for the callout by clicking on the listing for it. The listing will be highlighted.

✓ Go to the Re-Order arrows at the bottom of the pane.

✓ Click on the down arrow. The listing will move down one place with each click. Move the callout to the end of the animations so that it comes up last.

✓ Make sure the Start of the Motion Path animation is set to "After Previous" so that the action of sliding the second page out from under the first occurs as soon as the second slide comes up.

Chapter 6
Slides with Video and Audio Elements

Slides that contain video and audio elements can be made by anyone, so long as the video or audio clip is available in a digital format recognized by PowerPoint. Such slides will make your presentation truly multimedia and thereby heighten interest in the subject matter of your presentation. It will also help those who learn best by involving more senses, because sight and movement with sound appeals to both visual and aural learners. The method for making the slide is straightforward and very similar to the creation of slides using digital photos as discussed in Chapter 4.

6.1 Slides with video clips

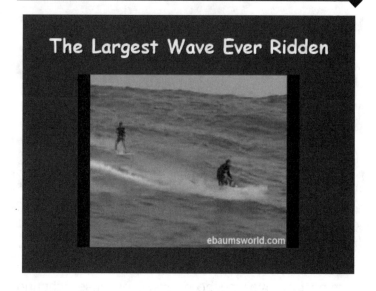

File type: The industry standard file type for video clips is MPEG, and these files have the extension name .mpeg or .mpg. Video clips may also have an AVI or MOV file type. For use in PowerPoint slides, AVI or MOV files must be converted to MPEG. The file conversion is a software operation that can be done using standard video editing software.

File folder: Videos are identified with a special icon so that you can tell by looking at a file listing which files contain video clips. Video files can be stored anywhere in your computer, or even on storage devices such as a CD, DVD, or memory stick. For PowerPoint slide shows, it is best to place video files to be played inside the same folder that contains the PowerPoint slide show. This insures the link between the two will always remain the same, no matter where you move the folder and the video will always play when you want it to.

A. Set up a Title Only slide and add the title.

✓ Go to the Formatting toolbar.

✓ Click on the New Slide button. This will display the Slide Layout Pane on the right side of the screen.

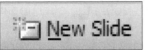

✓ Go to the Slide Layout Pane.

✓ Click on the Title Only slide layout option. A new blank slide is now on the screen.

✓ Add the title.

B. Add the video clip.

✓ Go to the Menu Bar.

✓ Click on the Insert Button. A drop-down menu will appear. It looks like this.

✓ Click on the Movies and Sounds option. A short listing of categories will appear.

✓ Click on Movie From File option. A dialog box will appear.

✓ Find the location of the file containing the video clip that you want. Click to highlight the file, and click OK at the bottom of the dialog box. A box containing the first frame of the video will appear on the screen.

✓ A message will appear saying: "How do you want the movie to start in the slide show?" Select the "When Clicked" choice because most of the time you will want to retain control of when the video plays. (Note: In PowerPoint 2002, the question is "Do you want your movie to play automatically in the slide show? If not, it will play when you click it." Select "No" as your answer.)

If you choose the "Automatically" option, the video will play as soon as the slide comes to the screen. This can be jarring for the viewer, who is not yet oriented to the subject.

You can get some control over the "Automatically" option with the Custom Animation option to delay the video for one or two seconds. (Menu Bar, Slide Show button, Custom Animation option, click the down arrow next to the listing for the video, click on the Timing option, and select a one-second or two-second delay.)

✓ Preview the video in the Normal View (the working screen). Put the mouse pointer inside the frame of video that is displayed on the screen and double click to start the video. Click if you want to stop the video before the end of the clip.

C. Add enhancements to the appearance of the slide.

1. Enlarge the video window.

The video will appear initially in a small window in the center of the slide. PowerPoint selects a size that provides good resolution for the video. This size may be too small for good viewing in the classroom.

To enlarge the video window, hold down the CTRL button while dragging a corner handle (this increases the size while keeping the window centered). You should not try to enlarge the video window to fill the entire slide, however, because the video will lose resolution (as you increase the size of the window) and look grainy.

If you have only one slide that has a video on it, dragging the corner handles until you get to the size you want will work well. If you have a number of slides with video clips, then you will probably want all the video windows to be exactly the same size. The Format Picture dialog box does this.

✓ Right click on the Video Window. A menu will appear.

✓ Click on the Format Picture option. A dialog box will appear.

✓ Click on the Size tab at the top. The display now looks like the screen above.

✓ Click on the checkboxes labeled "Lock aspect ratio" and "Relative to original picture size" if they are not already checked.

✓ Click on the up arrow next to the Height box to increase the size of the window for the video, or delete the current number and type in whatever size you want.

✓ Click on the OK button at the bottom of the dialog box.

✓ Using the Guides, position the resized window. See section 2.3(B)(1) on the Guides.

2. Put a frame around the window.

The video window acts like any other object. You can put a line border around it (Drawing Toolbar, Line Style button) and change the color of the border from the default black to any other color (Drawing Toolbar, Line Color button).

Consider using a shadow around the bottom and right edges of the window to make it appear to come off the page a bit (Drawing Toolbar, Shadow Style button).

3. Color the background of the slide (Formatting Toolbar, Background button) behind the video window.

D. Play the video as part of the slide show.

To play the clip as part of a slide show—

✓ Click on the Slide Show icon.

✓ Place the mouse pointer inside the video screen. You may have to move the mouse around a bit to bring up the pointer. Once you put the cursor inside the video screen it turns into a little white hand.

✓ Click once and the video will begin to play.

✓ Click again while the cursor is still within the video screen and the video will stop.

✓ Click again and the video will start again. You can stop and start the video this way as many times as necessary.

6.2 Slides with audio clips

File type: The digital sound files used with Power-Point slides are WAV files. Some music files come in MIDI format, which are generally very large files that will have to be converted to WAV files to be used with PowerPoint.

File folders: Audio clips are named and filed in the same way as video clips. See section 6.1.

A history teacher lecturing on the start of America's involvement in World War II might play President Roosevelt's famous address to the nation advising of the attack on Pearl Harbor.

The slide might look like this.

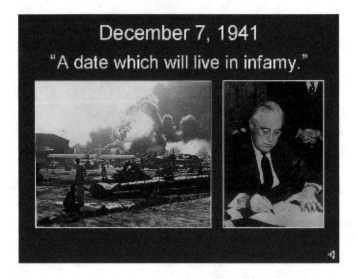

Create this slide by importing the photographs of the attack on Pearl Harbor and President Roosevelt signing the Declaration of War. See section 4.5(B). Add a two-line title. See section 4.2(B).

A. Import the sound file.

✓ Go to the Menu Bar.

✓ Click on the Insert button. A drop-down menu will appear.

✓ Click on the Movies and Sounds option. A subsidiary menu will appear. See section 6.1(B).

✓ Click on the Sound from File option. A dialog box will appear.

✓ Find the file that contains the sound clip of this speech.

✓ Click on the file name.

✓ Click OK at the bottom of the dialog box.

B. Position the sound icon.

PowerPoint puts a sound icon on the slide, usually somewhere in the middle. It looks like this.

 The icon has handles and can be moved to any position on the slide. It can also be made larger or smaller, depending on the needs of the display. To make the sound icon less noticeable to the viewer, give it a fill color (Drawing toolbar, Fill Color button) that is the same as the background of the slide and put it in a lower corner on the slide.

C. Specify how the sound is to be played.

You can either play the sound beginning on a mouse click, which allows control when the audio starts, or you can have the sound play automatically when the slide is displayed, just as with a video clip as mentioned in section 6.1(B). The same directions apply.

D. Play the sound.

To play the audio clip—

✓ Go to the View Bar.

✓ Click on the Slide Show button to bring the slide to the screen in its show mode. The sound icon will be visible in the location you have chosen.

✓ Place the mouse pointer over the icon. You may have to move the mouse around a bit to bring up the pointer. Once you put the mouse pointer over the icon, it turns into a little white hand.

✓ Click and the audio will play from start to finish. Unlike the video clip, you cannot stop and start the audio except by stopping the slide show.

Chapter 7
Slide Numbers and Notes

PowerPoint has an automated capability to add slide numbers, which may be useful for keeping track of the presentation and for providing students with supplementary materials. PowerPoint also allows you to add notes to your slides to remind you of points that you intend to make. These notes can be printed out or posted together with a thumbnail of the slide.

7.1 Slide numbers

You may want to put slide numbers on your slides so that you can find them in the slide show when working from hard copies or from notes. If you put slide numbers on the slides, they will also be on the printed copies.

PowerPoint provides a powerful tool to get to any slide in a slide show very quickly. When the slide show is running, type the number on your keyboard that corresponds to the slide number you want on the screen, and press ENTER. The software will take you instantly to that slide.

This means that, if you are working from notes while giving a lecture, you can skip from place to place in the slide show using your notes, which contain references to slide numbers. If students have printed out hard copies of the slides and have questions, they can refer to the slide number. The instructor can put the slide on the screen, and the entire class can then follow the discussion more easily.

To add slide numbers, do this—

A. Open the Header and Footer dialog box.

1. Go to the Menu Bar.

2. Click on the Insert button. A drop-down menu will appear.

3. Click on the Slide Number option. A dialog box will appear.

4. Click on the Slide tab at the top of the dialog box. The display in the dialog box will look like this.

The software has reserved three boxes at the bottom of the slide layout. They are shown in the Preview box at the lower right corner of the dialog box. The box at the bottom right is for the slide number. The box in the middle is for a footer. The box on the left is for the date and time.

The default settings have the Date and time box (fixed) checked and the Footer box checked. Both of these options leave blanks on the slide unless you type information into the dialog box.

The "Date and time" option has two suboptions. The date and time can be fixed by you (by typing a date into the box provided) or the date and time can be entered automatically by the system. A small down arrow next to the Update automatically box provides access to a menu of style choices.

The Footer option allows you to type in text that will appear as a footer on the slide. This might be the name of the course, the name of the instructor, the name of the slide show, or other information that should be on the slide. In most cases, however, the footer will be left blank.

The dialog box provides the option to apply the date and time and footer to every slide in the slide show, or just to individual slides.

B. Designate slide numbers.

1. Click on the small checkbox in front of the Slide Number option. A check mark will appear in the box.

2. Click on the Apply to All button in the upper-right corner.

The small box on the lower-right edge of the slide is now active and it will display a slide number, as assigned by the system. This will be the same slide number as appears on the Slides Pane or in the Slide Sorter View.

7.2 Slide notes

◆

The Normal View, or working screen where you construct your slides, has a Notes Pane at the bottom.

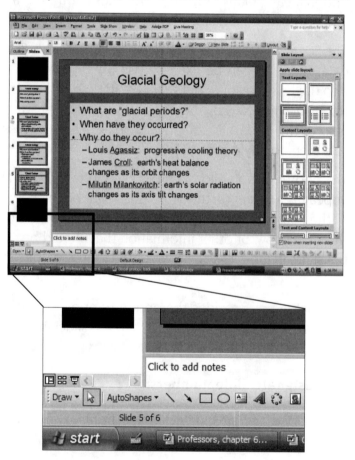

This expandable work area allows you to type in notes or import word processing material for any slide. Notes can contain ideas for lectures, information on source materials, possible follow-up points, or any other useful information.

A. Add notes.

- ✓ Go to the Notes Pane. The Notes Pane shows the label "Click to add notes."

- ✓ Move your mouse pointer to this label and click once with the left mouse button. The label will disappear, and the cursor will be blinking.

- ✓ Type in text.

The Notes Pane will hold up to one page of text.

B. Enlarge the Notes Pane.

If you have only a few lines of notes, the very small area at the bottom of the display will suffice. If you go beyond the allotted area, you can scroll down to read the rest of your notes.

If you have a substantial amount of material that you want to preserve with the slide show as notes for particular slides, you may want to expand the Notes Pane so that you can see it all while you are working.

To do this—

- ✓ Locate the gray border at the top of the Notes Pane.

- ✓ Put your mouse pointer over the border until its shape changes to two lines with an up arrow above and a down arrow below.

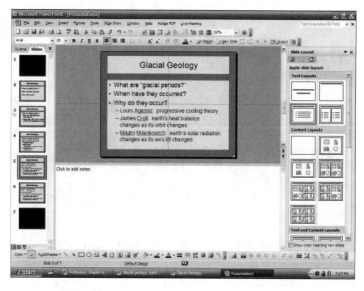

✓ Hold down the left mouse button and drag the border up. As you drag the border upward, the size of the slide will decrease. This gives you a preview of how your notes page will look when you print it out.

✓ When you have increased the area of the Notes Pane sufficiently, let up on the mouse button.

C. Format the text of notes.

You can use all of the normal formatting in your notes. If you want the formatting to apply to all of the text in the box, click on the border of the box to change it to a dotted border and then click on the button you need to get the formatting change. If you want the formatting to apply to only selected text (such as boldface applied only to a few words), highlight the text within the box and then click on the appropriate button:

✓ Font style and size

✓ Font color

✓ Emphasis with bold, italic, underline.

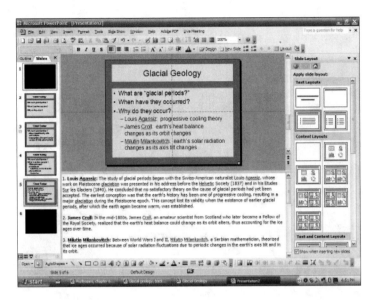

✓ Spacing and paragraphing

The normal SpellCheck functions will work when you are entering Notes.

D. The Notes Page.

The Notes Page is an automated way to create a hard copy printout for each of your slides with its associated notes.

1. Display the Notes Page.

To look at a Notes Page for a particular slide, do this—

✓ With the slide on your screen in the Normal View (the screen display in which you create your slides)—

✓ Go to the Menu bar at the top of the screen.

✓ Click on the View button. A drop down menu will appear.

✓ Click on the Notes Page option. The Notes Page will appear on your screen. It looks like the illustration below.

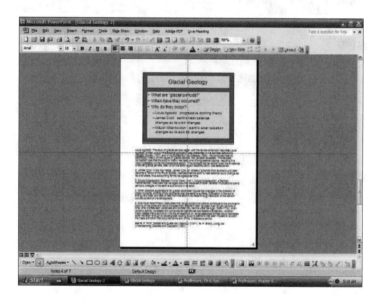

To go back to Normal View: Go to the View bar in the lower-left corner of the screen display, just above the Drawing toolbar. Click on the Normal View button, which is the one on the left side of the toolbar.

2. Increase the size of the type on the Notes Page.

The Notes Page is only one page long. If the AutoFit is turned on, the software will automatically reduce the type size if you exceed the amount of space available on the page.

To turn the AutoFit on:

✓ Go to the Menu bar.

✓ Click on the Tools option.

✓ Click on AutoCorrect Options.

✓ Click the AutoFormat As You Type tab.

✓ Click on the boxes labeled "AutoFit title text to placeholder" and "AutoFit body text to placeholder."

This will turn the AutoFit feature on with respect to your slides as well as your notes, so if you don't want to use it when you are constructing slides, remember to turn it off again.

To change the size of the Note Pane boxes:

You can change the size of the two boxes on the page—one for the thumbnail of the slide and one for the notes—to create more space for notes.

✓ Click on the box to activate it. Be sure that the dotted border is showing.

✓ Place your mouse pointer over a corner handle.

✓ Drag in the direction you want to go—outward to increase the size of the box, or inward to decrease the size of the box.

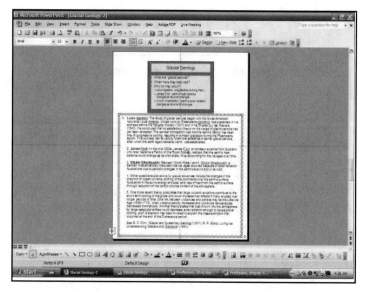

As you create more space, the size of the type will automatically be increased.

A smaller slide box, for example, can be moved toward the top of the page (click to activate the box, use the mouse pointer to drag the box) to create more room for a larger notes box.

To go back to the original layout: If you change the size of the slide box or the notes box and then decide you don't like the new layout, you can get back to the original layout this way—

✓ With the Notes Page on the screen—

✓ Go to the Menu bar.

✓ Click on the Format button. A menu will appear.

✓ Click on the Notes Layout option. A dialog box will appear.

✓ Click on the small box in front of the Master Layout option to check it.

✓ Click on OK. The original layout will reappear.

If you need a lot more space: If your notes are more than one page, you have two options:

✓ Create a new blank slide so that you will have a second Notes Page for the continuation of your notes.

✓ Transfer your Notes Page over to Word (see section 7.2(G)) where you will have as much space as you want.

3. Add "pictures" to the notes.

You can add to your notes anything that PowerPoint regards as a "picture." This includes photos, other illustrations, clip art, logos, and similar objects.

A picture or object that you add in the Notes Page view will appear on your printed Notes Page, but not when you are looking at your notes below the slide in Normal View. See section 7.3(C) on printing notes.

The changes, additions, and deletions you make on a particular Notes Page apply only to that Notes Page and the note text in Normal View.

4. Add color to the notes.

Normally, you will want to print your notes with black type on a white fill. If you decide to add font color or fill color, do it this way—

✓ With the Notes Page showing—

✓ Click on the border to change to a dotted border if the dotted border is not showing.

✓ Go to the Drawing toolbar.

✓ Click on the Fill Color or Font Color buttons and make your choices from the dialog boxes that appear.

If you want background color for your notes pages, go to the Formatting toolbar, click on the Background button, and make your choices from the dialog boxes that appear.

E. The Notes Master.

To have your style selections apply to all notes pages in the presentation, use the Notes Master.

To get to the Notes Master, do this—

✓ Go to the Menu bar at the top of the screen.

✓ Click on the View button. A menu will appear.

✓ Click on the Master option. Another menu will appear.

✓ Click on the Notes Master option. The Notes Master display will appear with a small toolbar to the right containing two options: Return to Normal View and Close Notes Master.

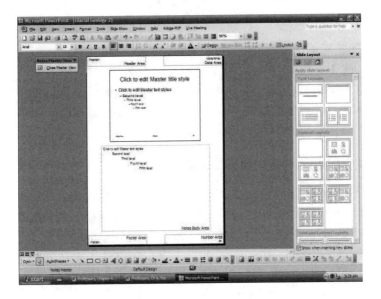

1. Headers and footers.

The Notes Master provides two headers and two footers. You might use the left header, for example, for the name of the course and the right header for the date on which you created the slide show. Place your mouse pointer in the header or footer box and click. You are now ready to type in content.

The headers and footers are boxes. You can change their size and shape using the dotted border.

2. Title box.

The Notes Master also provides a title style box. The only change you can make to the title style box is the size of the box. (Ignore the text within the title style box.) To change the size of all of the slide images on your notes pages, use the *corner handle* to make the standard box bigger or smaller. Then drag the box back into position. Use the corner handle to avoid distorting the image of the slide.

3. Text box.

The Notes Master displays a text box for your notes. Use the text style box if you want to change the font, for example, on all your notes. You can also change the size of the text box using the dotted border and any of the handles.

F. Displaying notes on a Web page.

If your school has a Web page, that can be a convenient way to make slide shows available to students. If you save your presentation as a Web page, your notes automatically display. Slide titles become a table of contents in the presentation, and your slide notes appear beneath each slide.

If you don't want your notes to display in the Web page, you can turn them off before you save the file as a Web page.

G. More layout options with Word.

You can send the notes pages to Microsoft Word from Microsoft PowerPoint for further formatting and print from there. For example, if you wanted to include two slides and their notes on a single page, you could apply that layout in Word.

To send your notes Word, do this—

   ✓ With your slide show open in PowerPoint—

   ✓ Go to the Menu bar.

   ✓ Click on the File button. A menu will appear.

   ✓ Click on the Send To option. A short menu will appear.

✓ Click on the Microsoft Word option. A dialog box will appear showing the layout options.

✓ Click either the "Notes next to slides" or "Notes below slides" check box.

7.3 Print slides and notes

When you print slides, they can be full size (one to a page) or in thumbnails (more than one to a page). Printing copies of slides is a very straightforward process. All of the necessary controls are in one place.

To print out your slides, do this—

A. Open the Print dialog box.

1. Go to the Menu Bar.

2. Click on the File button.

3. Click on the Print option. A Print dialog box will appear. It looks like this.

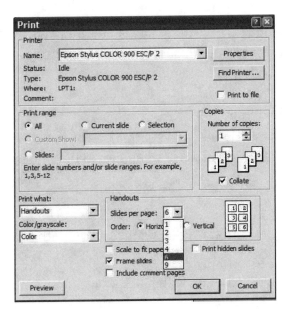

B. Print slides.

If you want to have a paper copy of the slides in your slide show, you can print them out using any color printer.

1. Printer and print quality.

At the top of the dialog box, the section labeled "Printer" shows the name of the printer you are currently using and provides the controls to change the printer.

To change to a different printer, click on the small down arrow to the right of the printer name box and select the printer you want to use.

To change the print quality—

- ✓ Click on the Properties button in the upper-right corner. A dialog box will appear.

- ✓ Click on the Paper/Quality tab. A dialog box will appear containing the options for paper size and quality.

The default setting for quality is not at high resolution, and you may need higher quality for printing slides if you intend to use them as handouts.

2. Print Range.

The Print Range area in the middle of the dialog box contains the choices for what should be printed.

- All the slides in the slide show that are currently active.

- The current slide that is active within a slide show.

- Selected slides within the slide show that are currently active. (You can do this in two ways—by highlighting the slide thumbnails or by designating the slide numbers.)

- A Custom Show. (The box to the right of this option allows you to locate the show that you want to print.)

3. Copies.

The control for the number of copies is a small up-down arrow on the right side of the dialog box.

If you print multiple copies, you can use the "Collate" feature to print in sets. When the Collate checkbox is checked, the printer will print all the pages of set 1, then all the pages of set 2, and so on. If the Collate checkbox is not checked, the printer will print all the copies of page 1, then all the copies of page 2, and so on.

4. Print format.

The area labeled "Print What" at the bottom of the dialog box allows you to designate the format in which you want to print the slides.

Slides can be printed in four formats—as slides, handouts, notes pages, or outlines.

- ✓ The slide format is one slide per 8½-x-11 printed page with a small margin around the edges.

- ✓ The handout format uses thumbnails of the slides and provides options of one, two, three, four, six, and nine thumbnails per page. If you choose the option for three slides on a page, the software automatically adds lined spaces to the right of each slide that can be used for handwritten notes.

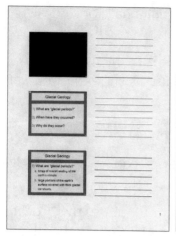 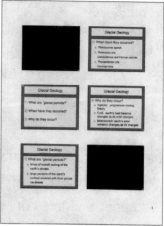

✓ The Notes Page provides one slide per page with a reduced size image of the slide at the top of the page (larger than a thumbnail) with your notes underneath as illustrated in section 7.2(D).

✓ The Outline View provides all of the text on the slides in an outline format.

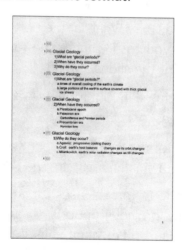

Slides can be printed in three color options—in color (for color printers), in grayscale (for black and white printers or to save color ink when working with drafts), and in pure black and white (usually not of use in educational applications).

Alternatively, if you have already set all of the controls, go to the Standard Toolbar, click on the Print button. This bypasses the Print dialog box.

C. Print notes.

To see how your notes will print and to see the full effect of your text formatting (such as font colors), use the Print Preview function.

- ✓ Go to the Menu bar.
- ✓ Click on the File button. A menu will appear.
- ✓ Click on the Print Preview option. The first slide will appear on the screen. The Print Preview toolbar will appear above it. The toolbar looks like this.

- ✓ Click on the small down arrow to the right of the box labeled "Print What" and a menu will appear.
- ✓ Click on the Notes Pages option. Check the spacing of the boxes, the size of the type, and the headers and footers. The Print Preview toolbar allows you to switch from Portrait to Landscape layout using the buttons immediately to the right of the Print What box.
- ✓ Click on the small down arrow to the right of the Options button on the toolbar. A menu will appear. Click on the Scale to Fit Paper option, which maximizes the size of the thumbnails making them somewhat more readable.

✓ When the layout is satisfactory, click on the Print button.

You can use the printed Notes Pages either as notes to yourself while you give your presentation, or, if they're notes you intend for your students, you can hand them out to accompany your slide show presentation.

Chapter 8
Making Presentations with Slides

After you have created the slides to use with your lecture, it is necessary to turn to some of the fundamentals of using PowerPoint slide shows in the classroom. The educator's task is in many ways made easier using presentations with slides. Following a few guidelines, set out in this chapter, will assist in making the most effective use of slides.

8.1 Sort slides

The first step in making a presentation with slides may be selecting the slides you want to use and putting them in the right order for the particular presentation you are about to make. PowerPoint provides several ways to do these steps; the easiest are described here.

A. Change the order of slides within a slide show.

If you have all the slides that you need within an existing slide show, but you need to move them around in order to meet the needs of a particular class, you can do it this way.

1. Make a copy of the entire slide show.

In most cases, it is better to make a copy of the slide show and work from the copy in order to protect against inadvertently losing any of your work. To do this—

✓ Open the slide show. See section 1.9(C)(D).

✓ Rename the slide show. (Go to the Menu bar and click on the File button; a menu will appear. Click on the Save As option, the Save As dialog box will appear with the current name of the file displayed in the File Name box at the bottom of the dialog box. Change the name. Click on the Save button in the lower right corner of the dialog box.)

When you rename the file, the new (renamed) version is on the screen and the old version is still on hand, unchanged in the folder where it was originally saved.

The Slide Sorter View displays all your slides in thumbnail format. The screen display looks like this.

2. Use the Slide Sorter View to move slides around within the slide show.

Once you have the Slide Sorter View on the screen, you can drag and drop your slides into the order you need. To do this—

✓ With your slide show open—

✓ Go to the View bar at the bottom left side of your screen.

✓ Click on the middle button which has four small squares (repre-senting slides) on it. The display will change automatically to the Slide Sorter View shown in the illustration above.

To move a slide—

✓ Click on the thumbnail of the slide to activate it. The thumbnail will have a blue border.

✓ Hold down the left mouse button and drag the slide to the new location. A long, thin-line marker will indicate where the slide will go given the current position of the mouse pointer.

To delete a slide—

✓ Click on the thumbnail to activate it.

✓ Press the DELETE key on your keyboard.

B. Borrow slides from another slide show.

Recycling slides will help speed your work. If you have slides that worked well in the past, and you can use all or parts of them in the new slide show, PowerPoint provides an easy way to borrow whole slides and put them into your current slide show.

Use the Slides Pane at the left side of the PowerPoint screen to indicate the place where you would like to put recycled slides into your slide show. To do this—

✓ Put the mouse pointer between the thumbnails of two slides.

✓ Click on this location. This puts a horizontal line where the recycled slide or slides will go.

Use the Slide Finder dialog box to locate the slides you want to recycle. To do this—

✓ Go to the Menu bar at the top of the screen.

✓ Click on the Insert button. A drop-down menu will appear.

✓ Click on the Slides From Files option. The Slide Finder dialog box will appear.

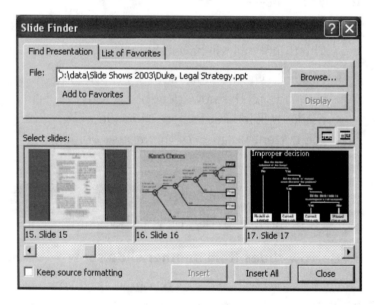

✓ Use the Browse button at the top right side of the box to display the directories and files on your computer.

✓ When you locate the file name of the slide show from which you want to take slides, click on it. This will display, in the top box labeled "File," the name of the file and its location in your directory.

✓ Click on the Display button. This will bring up one of two displays, either thumbnails (in the illustration on the previous page) or titles.

The display options are controlled by two small buttons just below the Display button on the right side of the dialog box. The thumbnail display button is on the left and the title display button is on the right.

Both display options have sliders (the slider on the thumbnail display is at the bottom) to advance through longer slide shows.

✓ Click on a thumbnail (or title) to be inserted. You can also select multiple slides (by holding down the CTRL key on your keyboard while you click on the slides you want) or all the slides in the slide show (by clicking on the Insert All button at the bottom of the dialog box).

✓ Decide whether you want to keep the formatting in the recycled slide. If you do, click on the "Keep source formatting" check box in the lower-left corner of the dialog box. If you want the background of the new slide show to be put into your recycled slides, leave this box unchecked.

✓ Click on the Insert button at the bottom of the dialog box. The recycled slide or slides will be copied into your current slide show at the location you selected on the Slides Pane.

8.2 Show slides

In most cases, you will be using a laptop computer to bring your slides to the classroom because it is not convenient to move a desktop computer. Similarly, in most instances, you will be using a digital projector to project your slides on a large projection screen or on a blank wall because the large plasma screens that are a possible alternative are expensive and are not set up for the height to width ratio used by PowerPoint slides.

Connect your laptop to the projector as directed in the instructions for the projector. Note that some projectors require that the projector be turned on first and connected to the computer before the computer is turned on. For more detailed instructions on using a digital projector, see *The Digital Projector and Laptop Computer* (NITA 2005).

PowerPoint has automated most of the features for showing your slides.

A. Open the slide show.

See section 1.9 (C)(D). The first slide will be on the screen.

B. Switch to the Slide Show View.

The slide show control is on the View Bar, which is a small tool-bar in the lower-left corner of  the screen, just above the Drawing Toolbar.

The View Bar's function is to switch among the three "views" available in PowerPoint—the Normal View (which is used to construct slides), the Slide Sorter View (which is used to move slides and add transitions), and the Slide Show View.

The button to switch to the Slide Show View is the last on the right. Click on this button to begin the slide show. The show will begin with whatever slide is on the screen at the time.

Alternatively, press the F5 button on your keyboard (usually on the top row of buttons), which will take you directly to Slide Show mode and will start at the first slide.

C. Advance the slides within the show.

Click the left mouse button once to advance to the next animation or the next slide.

Alternatively, use the SPACE BAR on the keyboard.

Alternatively, use a remote control. The projector may have a remote control that came with the unit. Remote controls that plug into the USB port of your computer can be purchased at any electronics store. See section G on remote controls.

D. End the slide show.

To leave the Slide Show View and go back to the Normal View—

✓ Click on the right mouse button. A menu will appear.

✓ Click on the End Show option. The view will switch back to the Normal View.

8.3 The educator and the "big screen"

A projection screen displaying compelling images competes for the attention of the students. If students are watching the screen, they are not watching the educator who is speaking. If they are not watching the educator, it may be that they are not listening to the educator either. Remember this rule: what is on the screen is likely to be much more interesting than you are. Therefore, when a large screen is used, be mindful of this competition for the students' attention and use the screen in a way that complements the oral presentation. And when you are finished with the points to be made using the screen display, blank the screen to re-direct attention back to you. See discussion of black slides at the start of Chapter 1 and in section 8.3(H)(2) below.

A. Position in relation to the projection screen.

The educator should stand somewhere near the front of the screen, but should not block the students' view of the screen. Try not to walk in front of the projector as this will block the image from reaching the screen and display the slide on your shirt front. Look directly at the students in the same way as if there were no visuals on the screen. The visuals reinforce the oral presentation; they do not replace it.

B. Position in relation to the laptop display screen.

When there is a need to consult the screen display, the educator usually will want to look at the laptop screen display rather than turning around to look at the big screen. Therefore, the educator's position should allow reference to the laptop by glancing down or sideways without moving or changing position for that purpose. Use a computer extension cord (available in most electronics stores) or a wireless setup, if necessary, to get the positioning right within the classroom layout.

C. Pointing to things on the screen.

The educator can point to things on the screen in several ways. The educator can walk to the screen, reach out, and point. This method has the advantage of being immediate and easy, but it will cause a shadow on the screen and block some of the image. A 3- to 5-foot long wooden or plastic pointer rod can be used to point at objects on the screen from a location to one side of the screen. A wooden yardstick or a simple half-inch wood dowel from the hardware store will do. This method causes a smaller and more manageable shadow on the screen. Walking around the classroom with a 3-foot stick in hand may not generate a positive image, so find a convenient place to store it when it is not needed.

Most projectors come with a remote control that includes a laser pointer. The pointer is an arrow or a red dot that shows up on the screen and is moved around the screen with a control on the remote that works like a mouse. Generally these pointers should *not* be used in a classroom. First, it is almost impossible to eliminate little hand motions which show up as jerky motions on the screen because they are magnified many times by the distance from the screen. Too much caffeine, too little sleep, or a measure of anxiety will become all too obvious with the rattling red dot. Second, many of these pointers are difficult to see—both too small and too light for classroom use.

PowerPoint has three built-in pen markers that can also be used to point out particular features of slide. When one of the pen markers is turned on, and the left mouse button is held down, the movements of the mouse will produce marks on the screen.

To prepare to use a marker—

✓ Go to the Menu Bar.

✓ Click on the Slide Show button. A menu will appear.

✓ Click on the Set Up Show option. A dialog box will appear. This shows the pen marker color in a box.

✓ Click on the small arrow next to the pen marker box to display the color palette. Choose a color.

Choosing a color before presenting the slide show allows you to experiment to see which color works best with the slides that you have and also obviates the need to display on the screen (before the students) a menu to get to a color choice.

To turn the marker on during a slide show—

✓ With the slide show running—

✓ Hold down the CTRL key and press the P key on the keyboard. Your mouse pointer will turn into a colored dot, and when you hold down the left mouse button and move the mouse, a line will appear on the screen.

To turn the marker off—

✓ Hold down the CTRL key and press the A key on the keyboard. Your mouse pointer will change back to the familiar arrow shape.

To save the markings you have made—

    ✓ When you close the slide show, a small dialog box will appear inquiring whether you wish to save the markings you have made or discard them.

In general, it is better to put markings and indicators on the slide during the slide preparation process and use animations to turn the markings on and off as you need them.

D. The educator's focus.

An important part of the classroom presentation is the way the educator directs his or her attention. The big screen can be a distraction in this regard. In general, an educator should not speak to or read material from the projection screen.

When an educator speaks, it should be to the students. The temptation to look at the big screen is strong because it is there and because its color and brightness demand attention. However, in order to look at the big screen, the educator usually has to turn away from the students. In this position, the educator is speaking at the screen and the words may be less distinct. In addition, the power of persuasion by looking directly at the audience is lost. The image shown on the projection screen is for the students. The educator needs to focus on the students and not on the projected slide. As noted above, the educator's position relative to the laptop allows a quick glance down at the laptop screen that will show what is being displayed on the big projection screen.

If an educator looks at the screen in class, it should be for the specific purpose of drawing all attention in the classroom to the particular item or words to which the educator is referring. Purposefully turning to the screen, and speaking (slowly) for effect, will emphasize the point.

E. Timing and pauses.

The essentials of basic public speaking—timing and pauses—apply in somewhat magnified ways when a educator is working with large-scale visual displays on a projection screen.

Educators need to give attention to the order in which the oral point and the visual point are made. Sometimes it is useful to display the visual before the oral explanation starts. For example, the educator displays the enlarged and labeled photo of the Malaspina Glacier in Alaska, pauses while the students look at the photo, and then says: "The Malaspina Glacier is the largest glacier in Alaska." More often, the timing works better if the educator makes the oral point first, shows the visual, pauses while the visual is absorbed, and then explains the point: "Let me show you a photo of the Malaspina Glacier in Alaska." Then bring up the image and continue the explanation. "This glacier extends about 50 miles from Mount St. Elias to the Gulf of Alaska and covers about 1,500 square miles, making it not only the largest glacier in Alaska but larger than the State of Rhode Island." This way, the visual reinforces the oral statement.

When using outlines or lists, the educator might state the first point, display the first point on the screen, then go on to explain it.

When slides are used to focus on a particular part of a document or photo, show the whole image on the screen without any changes or additions. Announce that you are going to blow up part of the image so everyone can see it better, then bring up the slide that has the enlargement and work from it.

Timing is important in not speaking ahead of slides— that is, getting the slide on the screen with the point to be made. Timing is equally important in not speaking about material on a slide after it has left the screen. This sometimes happens with outline slides when the educator clicks to the next slide before finishing the last point in the outline. To avoid this problem, use the end-of-slide signal boxes that are explained in section 2.5(11).

Pauses are important when making presentations that use significant visuals because the students become frustrated, and ultimately inattentive, if the educator rushes along, not giving them a chance to absorb what is on the screen. Always remember—this is the first time the students have seen this information, while you have lived with it the entire time you've been planning the lecture. While the technology allows the educator to put up many images in rapid succession, your goal should be "information-grasped-per-minute" and not "images-projected-per-minute." If anything, large screen graphics require that the presenter slow down from normally-paced oral explanations so that the audience is not left behind.

F. Orientation and anchoring.

Slide shows often have visual images flying onto the screen in rapid fashion without any explanation of what is being displayed. Because images can be put on the big screen so easily and quickly, educators sometimes miss the point that, with this wonderful technology, orientation for the viewer has become even more important. The educator's mantra should be "orient, orient, orient." Slow down, and take the students through each slide carefully. Make sure they appreciate what the slide is and what it shows.

One way to accomplish a good orientation is to start at the top and go down through the slide explaining the details. If the students see early on in the presentation that the instructor will orient them to each image that is presented, their anxiety level will drop and they will concentrate on the slides, comforted that sufficient time will be spent to explain what the slides are and why they are significant.

When a slide depicting a document or photo is about to appear on the screen for the first time, it is important that the students know what is about to occur. When a portion of a document or photo will be displayed so that the educator can deal with particular facts, the entire document or photo should appear first. This "anchors" the portion that will be discussed by reference to the "whole thing." Otherwise, if what first appears is a highlighted, underlined, boxed-in, blown-up, or called-out document or photo, you may confuse the students.

Start with the plain, unadorned slide. Then announce how you are going to change or emphasize the slide. A marked "anchor" should be put on the slide showing the location from which the excerpt will be drawn. In using document slides, the text to be enlarged may be framed with a small box. Then the excerpt can be shown in a blowup or callout that is placed over a portion of the slide or alongside the slide. This way, the students know that the callout came from a particular place in a specified document.

G. Working with a remote control.

A digital projector is just a tool in a classroom. It should not be a center of attention. The controls for a projector are very simple and almost foolproof. The most difficult part of using the equipment is having enough confidence so that the focus is on what is being said, not what is being done at the controls. The educator is still the messenger, with the technology just another visual aid.

1. Light hand on the controls.

An educator's angst at using presentation technology is often expressed most clearly in the mannerisms accompanying the use of the controls. Whether pressing a button on a handheld remote or tapping the spacebar, the educator needs to appear to be at ease with the task. Twitching, clutching, and nervous glances at the equipment expecting imminent failure make the students aware that the educator is uncomfortable with the equipment. They expect the kind of seamless ease that they see on television, and they are distracted by anything less. Comfort at the controls comes with practice. Do not give your lecture supplemented with PowerPoint slides for the first time in front of your class. Get the timing down ahead of time.

2. Awareness of the receivers.

A remote will operate very reliably if its signal is within the range of the receiver on the projector. (The remote also has to have adequate battery power to send signals when prompted by a click on one of its buttons.) The receivers are located at specific points in the projector case or are attached to a USB port on the laptop.

An RF (radio frequency) remote (with the receiver either in the projector or the laptop) is the easiest to manage. It reaches the receiver from all 360 degrees around the location of the receiver and its normal range is about 50 feet.

An IR (infrared) remote (with the receiver in the projector) is the equipment usually supplied by manufacturers. The normal range of an IR receiver is about 25 feet within a 30 to 90 degree angle. So the educator operating the remote must have a mental picture of this range and stay within it. It does no good to aim the remote at the left side of the projector if the only receivers are in the back and front of the unit. Some educators paste green dots on the projector to remind themselves of the location of the IR receivers.

Some remotes will operate either by aiming at a receiver or by aiming at the projection screen (which bounces the signal back to the receiver). However, aiming at the screen is usually not a good choice in the classroom. First, the screen is usually behind the educator or to one side. So the educator has to turn back to the screen, which means turning away from the students. Second, using the screen reduces the distance at which the remote will operate. For example, if the range for optimum operation is 25 feet from the receiver, then the distance to the screen *and* back to the receiver has to be 25 feet or less.

If you are going to be presenting with slides regularly, the radio frequency (RF) "clicker" is preferable to the infrared (IR) unit. An RF clicker costs under $100 and works with any laptop with a USB port.

3. Unobtrusive aiming.

Inexperienced users often reach out toward the projector with the remote in hand as if pointing a gun. Keeping the remote in hand and simply clicking from a relaxed position not far from the body is better. Stretching out to point the remote will not make it work any better. Practice is very important in this regard. With practice, it becomes second nature to just click the remote from a relaxed arm and hand position.

4. Know your backup controls.

Occasionally a remote does not work. You click on a button and nothing happens. If you are using an infrared (IR) remote, there may be some object between you and the receiver on the projector. If you are using a radio frequency (RF) remote, you may have wandered out of the range of the receiver. Or, with either kind of remote, if you have forgotten to replace the batteries at reasonable intervals (specified in the directions for your remote), you may be out of power.

Whatever the cause of the remote's failure to respond, you have a ready alternative: you can use one of the sets of controls on the keyboard of the laptop. The spacebar is usually the easiest because it is the largest. Whichever backup control you prefer, just go there without any comment or fluster, and move on to the next slide. Use the next break to figure out what is wrong with the remote.

H. On-screen helpers.

Knowledgeable educators use several on-screen helpers to make the presentation move more smoothly.

1. Slide numbers.

Every slide should have the slide number displayed in the lower right-hand corner. That way, any time you look at the slide, or the students look at the display, the slide number is readily available. For instructions on adding this element to a slide, see section 6.1.

If you provide supplementary materials to the students to accompany the lecture, they can be keyed to the slide numbers.

2. Black slides.

A slide that is colored entirely black will cause the screen to go blank. There are always times during any presentation that the educator needs to have the focus be entirely on the oral presentation. To make the screen's competition disappear, a black slide can be used to turn off the image. These slides can be placed strategically throughout the slide show. The black slide prevents the students from losing focus on the educator. Left to their own devices, people tend to look at a television-type picture when it is available. The black slide brings them back to the oral statements.

The "B" key: One additional control on the laptop keyboard is available when using PowerPoint slides. Tapping the B key will blank the screen (in the same way as a black slide). Tapping the B key again will return to the previous display.

The "Home" key: Another keyboard control is available to get to a black slide at any time. If the first slide in the show is a black slide, tapping the Home key will take you there.

The "number+Enter" control: Any slide can be displayed by typing the number of the slide (within the slide show) and tapping the Enter key. That control will take you directly to the slide from wherever you are in the slide show. For example, if you used the Home key to get to a black slide, you would then need to use the "number+Enter" control to get back into the slide show at the correct slide.

Black slides are especially important at the beginning and at the end of any slide show. A black slide at the beginning of the slide show allows the educator to set up the computer and projector and keep all the equipment on until it is ready to be used, but without anything on the screen. A black slide at the end of the slide show is a crisp way to take the slides off the screen. If the last slide is left on the screen, it may not match the oral ending that is planned. If the educator goes beyond the last slide, with no black slide in place, the laptop will display the thumbnails of all the slides for the students to see. The black slide is a fail-safe mechanism.

3. End-of-slide signal boxes.

Some slides may have several elements and animations that make those elements appear seriatim. In the simplest example, an outline may be animated so that one point comes up at a time while the educator is talking. In order to avoid going to the next slide before you are finished with the current slide, you need to know when the last element has appeared on the current slide—because when that has happened, the next click is going to take you to another slide.

Insert a small white or colored box (or dot) in the lower right corner of the slide. See section 2.5(11). Animate the signal so that it appears with the last item on the slide (using a "With Previous" animation) or so that it appears on a click when everything else on the slide is done. This will help make sure that you don't advance to the next slide prematurely. When you see the dot appear, you know that the next click will bring you to the next slide, so you can be sure you have finished saying everything you intended to say about the current slide before going on.

The end-of-slide signal is small enough to be unobtrusive. Most students will never notice it when it appears. But, because the educator knows where to look for it, the little shape becomes an easy signal to follow.

8.4 Dealing with malfunctions and glitches

At some point during a class, electronic equipment may fail. As a general rule, the more equipment is being used, the less likelihood of some malfunction or glitch. Experienced educators report that failure almost always happens (if it is going to happen) on the first day of class, or the first day of the week. Once operational in a particular setting, equipment rarely malfunctions.

Fear of malfunction keeps some educators from even starting to use the equipment. That is shortsighted. Equipment failures are not difficult to deal with.

A. Attitude and practice.

In order to deal with potential equipment failure, the educator needs to have the confidence that any equipment failure can be overcome successfully without adverse effect on the class.

When equipment fails during class, the single most important thing a educator can do is just go on with whatever is happening without *any* comment or acknowledgment, until an opportune time comes to take a short break.

A smile is a solid way to glide over mistakes and problems with equipment. If you can regard your own problems with humor, the students will not think anything important has happened. If something happens that you cannot get around, point it out (thus putting it on your own shoulders), and then just get on with what you wanted to say.

B. Planning and prevention.

Any use of technology in a classroom benefits from planning and steps to prevent possible malfunctions. In the case of a digital projector setup driven by a laptop computer, these steps are easy to accomplish.

The projector has a bulb that can wear out. Every projector manufacturer provides the expected life of the bulb (in hours of use) and the projector itself carries a calculation of how many hours have already been used. The bulb usage number is usually on the status menu. Ask to have a spare bulb available for backup.

The remote control operates on batteries. You should put fresh batteries in the remote at intervals recommended by the manufacturer. Have replacement batteries in the projector's carry case.

The laptop may also operate on its battery. You should have the battery fully charged when you start and be able to plug into a power outlet quickly if necessary.

Chapter 9
PowerPoint Refresher

This chapter contains refresher information if you need to check on any aspect of setting up PowerPoint for use in making educational displays. Beyond the basics covered here, there are many important shortcuts available in the PowerPoint software that can be useful for creating educational slides. See *PowerPoint* 2003: 50 *Great Tips for Better, Easier Slides* (NITA 2005).

9.1 Basic Vocabulary

You can use PowerPoint without knowing all of the somewhat arcane vocabulary that appears in many manuals. In this book, we have attempted to stick to plain English. However, there are certain terms that are key to the use of the software, and they appear frequently in the chapters of this book. We have defined each of them here.

A. Windows vocabulary.

Button: Areas on the screen, typically located on a toolbar and defined by a word label or icon, where you can click to activate a software function.

Click on [something]: Place the mouse pointer in the designated area, press once on the left button on the "mouse" device connected to the computer, then release the button quickly. Occasionally, the software requires a right click (press the right mouse button and release). When a right click is required, the text will specifically point that out. Otherwise, "click on" always means the left mouse button.

Cursor: The cursor is a blinking boldfaced vertical line of a size similar to the mouse pointer that appears only when the software expects you to be typing something—letters, numbers, or symbols. When you start typing, the first letter appears at the cursor's location. The cursor appears in only one way. It is always a blinking vertical line. (The cursor always blinks; the mouse pointer never does.)

Drag [something]: Place the mouse pointer on an object. Hold down the left mouse button and move the mouse in the direction you want to move the object. The object will be "dragged" to a new location.

Minimize/maximize: The Windows software always presents three control buttons in the upper-right corner of the screen.

Mouse pointer: When you move a "mouse" device connected to a computer, a small indicator appears on the screen showing the current location to which the mouse device is "pointing." The indicator is usually an arrow shape, but can be other shapes depending on what the software is currently being asked to do.

Pane: Area on the screen, typically wide panels at the left and right of the screen display, containing a number of menu items or a related set of controls.

Toolbar: Area on the screen, typically long, narrow horizontal "bars" at the top and bottom of the screen display containing a number of icons or "buttons."

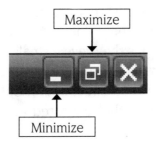

Windows can make the current window (for example, displaying PowerPoint) disappear, leaving only an icon representing this window on the blue Task Bar along the bottom of the screen. This is the "minimize" function. When you want that window back, you can go back to the Task Bar, click on the icon, and it will reappear.

Windows will also make the current window increase in size so that it takes up the entire screen (if it does not do that already). This is the "maximize" function. If the maximize button shows two squares, the screen display is already at its maximum and clicking on this button will reduce the window size so that other windows can be seen. If the maximize button shows one square, the screen display is not at its maximum and clicking on this button will enlarge it.

Windows will also close the program altogether. This is the red button with the white X.

Default: Windows and the software running under it will do things in a certain way if they are not told to do something else. The "default" option is what the software will choose if left to its own devices.

Dialog box: This is a display that provides a number of interrelated choices. Instead of having to use buttons located on different toolbars, all the tools for a particular set of operations are in the dialog box.

Menu: This is a display that provides a list of options. Options that have three dots after them will lead to a dialog box. Options that have a small arrow after them will lead to another menu. Options that have neither dots nor an arrow are direct action options and when you click on them, the requested action will happen automatically.

B. PowerPoint vocabulary.

Activate (an object or a slide): PowerPoint manages the operations that go into preparing a slide by requiring you to designate where you want to work next. You activate the area where you will be working by highlighting it (in the case of text) or clicking on it (in the case of boxes or other objects).

Object: This term includes shapes (such as a box, rectangle, or circle), lines, documents, photographs, and diagrams placed on a slide as a part of carrying out the design of the slide. Objects can be moved, resized, aligned with other objects, filled with text, colored, given borders, and animated in order to deliver the slide's intended message more effectively.

Slide: This is a single visual aid, constructed with Power-Point, which can be displayed on a computer monitor or (through a digital projector) on a projection screen.

Slide show: This is a collection of slides intended for a specific purpose or a presentation.

View: This is a screen display. PowerPoint does three basic things: create slides, organize individual slides into slide shows, and display slide shows. It has three Views, one for each of these purposes. The Normal View is used to create slides, the Slide Sorter View is used to organize slide shows, and the Slide Show View is used to display finished slide shows.

9.2 Setting up for educational slides

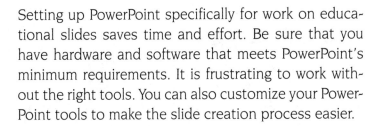

Setting up PowerPoint specifically for work on educational slides saves time and effort. Be sure that you have hardware and software that meets PowerPoint's minimum requirements. It is frustrating to work without the right tools. You can also customize your Power-Point tools to make the slide creation process easier.

A. Hardware and software requirements.

1. Hardware.

PowerPoint does not require sophisticated computer equipment. You need—

- A laptop or other computer that has a Pentium III processor or the equivalent; at least 128 MB of RAM and at least 15 MB of free storage space on the hard disk, which is needed to store the slides created in each chapter.

- A mouse plugged into the computer. This is useful even if the computer is a laptop.

- A CD drive in the computer or attached to it.

2. Software.

You need this software on your computer—

- Windows XP. PowerPoint can run on prior versions of Windows, but all of the illustrations in this book are made using XP.

- PowerPoint 2003, which can be purchased as a stand-alone program or as part of the Office 2003 suite. You can also use PowerPoint 2002, which is quite similar to PowerPoint 2003, but it is easier to just upgrade with a download from Microsoft's Web site.

B. Open the software.

To turn PowerPoint on, follow these steps.

1. Turn the computer on.

2. Click on the green Start button. It is located at the very bottom-left corner of the screen. A menu will appear above the Start button.

3. Click on the Programs option on this menu. Another menu will appear to the right listing all the programs available on your computer.

4. Move the mouse pointer to the Microsoft PowerPoint option on this programs menu. Click on this option. The opening screen will appear.

To create a handy shortcut so that you will be able to start up PowerPoint from your desktop display, *right* click on the PowerPoint option on the programs menu. A small menu will appear. Click on the "Send to" option; another small menu will appear, and click on "Desktop." The small PowerPoint icon will appear on your desktop display. Clicking on this icon will launch the PowerPoint program.

C. Check the key parts of the display.

You should check the basic parts of the screen display to be sure all the tools you need for building educational slides are on the screen. This saves time later on. If any are missing or out of place, subsection 9.2(E) describes how to retrieve and move them.

1. Windows bars.

At the very top of the screen there is a blue bar, the Title Bar, that tells you what program is currently active and the name of the file that is open.

Immediately below the blue bar is the standard Windows Menu bar. It is easily recognized because its buttons have names (File, Edit, View, and so on) rather than icons.

At the very bottom of the screen, there is another blue bar, the Task Bar, that at the left has the START button; across the middle it shows what programs are running, and at the right it usually displays the current time and other icons indicating shortcuts to software available on the computer.

Just above the bottom blue bar is the standard gray Windows Status bar that shows the page or slide and details about any template that is being used.

2. PowerPoint toolbars.

The basic screen display also has four toolbars—the Standard and Formatting toolbars at the top and the Drawing and Picture Toolbars at the bottom. Toolbars can be moved and changed. You need to check to be sure all are displayed in the proper locations.

The Standard and Formatting toolbars should be displayed on two rows at the top of the screen display under the Menu Bar. To accomplish this, see section 9.2(E)(4). The left half of these two toolbars (they are too long to display in their entirety) looks like this—

The Drawing and Picture toolbars should be displayed on one row above the Status Bar.

The Drawing toolbar looks like this.

The Picture toolbar looks like this.

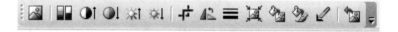

If these toolbars are missing or out of place, section 9.2(E) describes how to restore and move them.

In addition, PowerPoint has one bar—the View Bar—located in the lower-left corner (usually just above the Drawing Toolbar), which is basic to the PowerPoint software and does not move or change. It looks like this.

If there are additional toolbars displayed (other than the four shown in the illustration), close them. Section 9.2(E)(3) describes how to do that. PowerPoint has fifteen toolbars, but other than the basic four (described above) all are for very specialized purposes and not usually needed.

3. PowerPoint panes.

The principal panes are two vertical panels that appear at the left edge and right edge of the screen containing tools arranged in ways to help you work more efficiently. If the panes are not showing on your screen, go to subsection D below, which describes how to restore them. If they are narrower than the panes shown in the illustration, go to subsection D, which describes how to adjust them.

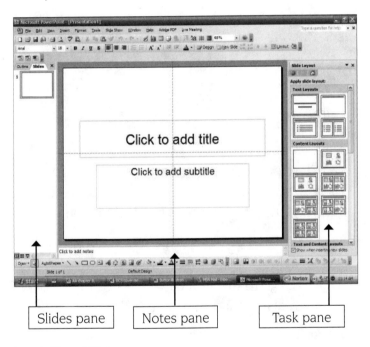

| Slides pane | Notes pane | Task pane |

D. Adjust the panes.

The left side of the screen has the *Slides/Outline Pane* (usually called the Slides Pane because the most frequently used panel displays thumbnails of all the slides in the slide show you are working on). The right side of the screen has the *Task Pane*. This is a housing for ten separate panes, each of which presents specialized controls for particular tasks. The bottom of the screen has the *Notes Pane*. This provides an area where you can record notes, ideas, or other information about a slide.

Each of the panes can be adjusted. They can be removed from the display, restored to the display, and adjusted in size on the display. Instructions are set out below.

1. Add a pane that is missing.

Each of the main panes can be restored to the screen display at any time.

Add the Slides Pane

  ✓ Go to the Menu Bar.

  ✓ Click on the View button. A drop-down menu will appear.

  ✓ Click on the Normal option at the top of the menu. This will restore all of the panes usually present in the Normal View, including the Slides Pane.

  ✓ Click on the Slides tab at the top of the pane.

Alternatively, go to the View bar at the bottom *left side* of the screen display and click on the Normal button.

Add the Task Pane

  ✓ Go to the Menu Bar.

  ✓ Click on the View button.

  ✓ Click on the Task Pane option. This will restore the Task Pane.

2. Adjust the width of a pane.

✓ Move the mouse pointer over the border of the pane that is next to the main area in the center of the screen. As the mouse pointer hovers over the border, it will turn to a two-arrow shape.

✓ Hold down the mouse button and drag the border so that the pane is wider or narrower.

When the pane is narrowed, the content remains the same. Use the scroll bar at the right side of the pane to scroll down to content on the longer, narrower display.

3. Close a pane that is not needed.

Close the Slides Pane and Task Pane

✓ Each of these two panes has a small Close button at the top right, marked with an X. Click on this Close button and the pane will disappear. This is sometimes useful if you need more work room on the screen for the slide.

Some who work with PowerPoint prefer to close the Task Pane when it is not needed for a specific task at hand. (It can be accessed quickly to perform a task related to the work on the screen display by activating the object and *right* clicking to bring up a menu.) Closing the Task Pane frees up considerable space on the screen display for the central pane in which work on slides is done.

Close the Notes Pane

✓ The Notes Pane can be "closed" by dragging its top border down to the bottom of the screen display.

If you work with PowerPoint often, and do not have a need to record notes about the slides, closing the

Notes Pane increases the available work space on the screen display.

E. Adjust the toolbars.

Four toolbars should be on the screen display—the Standard and Formatting toolbars at the top of the screen display and the Drawing and Picture toolbars at the bottom of the display. The Standard and Formatting toolbars should be displayed on separate rows (because they are quite long and it is advantageous to have all their buttons showing), and the Drawing and Picture toolbars should be displayed on one row (because they are short and will fit on one row with all their buttons showing).

1. Add a toolbar that is missing.

    ✓ Go to the Menu Bar.

    ✓ Click on the View button. A drop-down menu will appear.

    ✓ Click on the Toolbars option. A dialog box listing all of the available toolbars will appear. The ones displayed on the screen will have a check mark.

    ✓ To add a toolbar, click on its checkbox, a check mark will appear, and the toolbar will appear on the screen.

2. Move a toolbar to a new position.

A toolbar may show up on the right or left side of the screen (instead of at the top or bottom), in a floating position in a random place on the screen, or above or below another toolbar. You can move any toolbar to a different position.

Each toolbar has a move handle that allows you to drag the toolbar to a new location. The handle is located at the far left of the toolbar, just in front of the first button. It is a small dashed vertical bar that looks like this enlarged version.

✓ Move the mouse pointer over the toolbar move handle.

✓ Hold down the left mouse button.

✓ Drag the toolbar to the position where you want it to be located. Let up on the left mouse button, and the toolbar should lock into place.

3. Close a toolbar that is not needed.

Use the method for adding toolbars and uncheck the box in front of its name. The toolbar will disappear from the screen display.

If the computer and software have been used by others, it is usually a good idea to adjust the toolbars. This makes it easier to follow the directions in this book because the illustrations will look like your screen display.

4. Put the Standard and Formatting Toolbars on separate rows.

The Standard Toolbar and the Formatting Toolbar can sit on the same row at the top of the screen, but if they do, there is not room for all their buttons. This is not a problem because there is a method to add and remove buttons (see section 9.2(E)(5)), but it can be annoying and time consuming not to have the buttons you need displayed at all times. If you put them on separate rows, they can be displayed with all their buttons.

To do this—

✓ Go to the Menu Bar (located just under the blue Title Bar at the top of the screen).

✓ Click on the Tools button. A drop-down menu will appear.

✓ Click on the Customize option on the menu. A dialog box will appear showing a number of choices for customizing the way the PowerPoint screen works.

✓ Click on the Options tab at the top of the dialog box.

✓ Look at the small checkbox that says "Show Standard and Formatting toolbars on two rows." It should be checked. If not, click on it to check it.

✓ Click on the Close button at the bottom of the dialog box. The toolbars should now be on two rows, with the Standard Toolbar on top and the Formatting Toolbar underneath.

5. Reset each toolbar and display all buttons.

Buttons can be moved around on a toolbar and, if your computer and software have been used by someone else, it is a good idea to reset the toolbars to their default configuration. However, the default configuration does not display all the buttons you will need, so you should take one extra step to get them all into the toolbar as it is displayed on the screen.

To reset the toolbar, do this—

✓ Go to the Standard Toolbar.

✓ Look at the very end of the toolbar. There will be a small down arrow. Click on it. A small two-item menu will appear.

✓ Click on the Add or Remove Buttons option. Another small two-item menu will appear.

✓ Click on the Standard option. A dialog box showing all of the buttons on the Standard Toolbar will appear. If there is a check mark in the small box in front of the name of the button, then the button is currently displayed on the toolbar.

✓ Go to the very bottom of the list. Click on the listing that says Reset Toolbar.

This will put the buttons in their default (or standard) order and display all of the most commonly used buttons. Some buttons that are used infrequently will not be checked.

To display and have available *all* the toolbar's buttons, do this—

✓ Follow the steps above to get to the dialog box.

✓ Move your mouse pointer over the first name of a button that is unchecked. The name of the button and its icon will be highlighted.

✓ Click on it. A check mark will appear indicating that the button has been added to the toolbar. Check for each unchecked button on the list.

✓ When you have checked all of the buttons, click outside the box. DO NOT click the Reset Toolbar button at the bottom of the box for that will return to the default setting and eliminate some of the selections you just made.

Go through these same steps for each of the other three principal toolbars on your screen (Formatting, Drawing, and Picture).

F. Adjust the AutoSave setting.

The AutoSave function operates in the background, as you are working, to save your work automatically. It turns itself on, does the Save procedure, and turns itself off without affecting any work that is ongoing. The AutoSave function works at set intervals. The default setting is 10 minutes. Because PowerPoint slides often involve detailed work, the loss of which could be very disruptive, it is useful to have the AutoSave function operate every 1 minute instead of every 10 minutes. To do this—

- ✓ Go to the Menu bar at the top of the screen display.

- ✓ Click on the Tools button. A menu will appear.

- ✓ Click on the Options listing. The Options dialog box will appear.

- ✓ Click on the Save tab at the top of the dialog box.

- ✓ Click on the small down arrow next to the box labeled "Save AutoRecover info every ___ minutes" and put 1 minute in the box.

- ✓ Click on OK at the bottom of the box.

G. Increase the number of Undos.

The Undo function is very useful in making slides. Instead of starting over again, you can just go back a few steps to where you were when the wrong path was taken.

You can set the number of "undos" your system will provide this way—

- ✓ Go to the Menu bar.

✓ Click on the Tools button. A menu appears.

✓ Click on the Options choice. A dialog box appears.

✓ Click on the Edit tab.

✓ Go to the Undo section in the lower part of the box.

✓ Use the small up arrow to set the maximum number of undos.

H. Adjust other settings.

PowerPoint allows you to specify how the features displayed on the screen will appear or act. It is frustrating to try to do some PowerPoint operation only to have the computer not cooperate because a setting tells it to do something else.

These settings are very easy to adjust, and the directions and illustrations in earlier chapters assume that the settings are as recommended in this section.

1. Bring up the Options dialog box.

Most of the convenient options for educational slides are listed on a display that you can find this way—

✓ Go to the Menu Bar. This is the bar right under the blue bar at the top of the screen.

✓ Click on the Tools button. A drop-down menu will appear.

✓ Click on the Options button. A dialog box will appear.

2. Activate the View tab settings.

✓ Click on the View tab at the top of the dialog box.

✓ Check all the boxes. Do this by moving your mouse pointer over each small square box and clicking on it.

✓ Click on the OK button at the bottom of the dialog box.

9.3 PowerPoint controls

PowerPoint provides controls for all of its functions in its panes and on its toolbars. There are a few key things to understand with respect to work on Power-Point slides.

A. PowerPoint's alternative ways of doing things.

PowerPoint often provides two, three, or even four alternate ways of doing the same thing. In general, for any given action or function, you could use a button control, a mouse shortcut through the *right* mouse button, or a keyboard shortcut. Depending on work styles, different people prefer one or the other of these alternatives.

In this book, the descriptions and illustrations focus on the easiest and most generally applicable method for most beginners. Many of the recommended controls are screen controls where you click on a button on the screen to initiate an action. A few are keyboard controls where you hold down the CTRL key and press another key to initiate an action. Occasionally, a right click mouse control is the easiest alternative.

For mouse controls, the left mouse button produces action; the right mouse button produces options—

usually a menu from which you can choose what you want to do.

B. Pointers.

The cursor and the mouse pointer perform different tasks, and the instructions in this book will often direct you to use one or the other.

1. Cursor.

The cursor appears only when the software expects you to be typing something—letters, numbers, or symbols. When you start typing, the first letter appears at the cursor's location. The cursor appears in only one way. It is always a blinking vertical line. (The cursor always blinks; the mouse pointer never does.) You can move the cursor to a new location in three ways. The first is to put your mouse pointer at the desired spot and click on the left mouse button to position the cursor. The second is to use the keyboard's arrow keys. The third is to use the keyboard's tab key.

2. Mouse pointer.

The mouse pointer is used for functions other than typing—activating buttons, menus, options, and dialog box choices, for example. The pointer can take a number of shapes, as shown on the next page, depending on what the software is being asked to do. It may be a single-headed arrow, a double-headed arrow (pointing up and down, sideways, or crosswise), a four-point arrow, an I-beam, an hourglass, a hand, a cross, and other shapes.

Common Mouse Pointer Shapes

One-arrow	Selects buttons and menu options	
Two-arrow	Drags handles to change the shape of boxes	
Four-arrow	Drags things to another place	
Cross	Indicates where shapes will be placed	
Crop	Changes the shape of pictures	

C. Borders.

Sometimes you need to look closely at the borders of boxes or other objects on the screen because the pattern on the border signals what can be done with the box as long as the current border is showing. The border may be hatched or dotted, and the box will respond differently depending on which it is.

1. Hatched border.

A hatched border is made up of small diagonal lines. This border has only one purpose. You can type in the box or edit what you have typed.

2. Dotted border.

A dotted border is made up of many small dots. When this border is active, you can work on text (edit, color, change typeface and type size), change fill and line col-

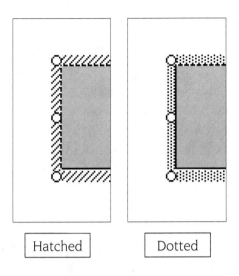

Hatched	Dotted

ors, move, resize, and copy the box. Any text within the box is automatically activated and ready to be worked on. It does not have to be highlighted in order to use text buttons (font, font color, bold, italic, underline, shadow, and other text effects). However, all the text in the box will be changed in the same way.

3. Switch from one border to the other.

Put the mouse pointer anywhere on the border and click on it. The border will change. In some cases, for instance, if you are working in a box with a dotted border and you start to type in additional words, Power-Point will switch borders automatically.

D. Handles.

A handle is a control that allows you to move part or all of an object. PowerPoint provides three sets of handles: sizing handles, rotate handles, and perspective handles. The sizing and rotate handles are most useful for litigation purposes.

1. Sizing handles.

The sizing handles are embedded in the border of a box or other shape. You can see the small circles in the illustrations of box borders. These are sizing handles. You use handles by putting your mouse pointer over them and (after the mouse pointer changes to a two-arrow shape indicating it is ready to move the object), holding down the mouse button and dragging the handle.

✓ Middle handles.

The handles in the middle of the top and bottom margins change height. The handles in the middle of the side margins change width.

✓ Corner handles.

The handles in the corner change height and width at the same time to keep the object proportionally the same although its absolute size is increased or decreased.

2. Rotate handle.

The rotate handle is a small, round green handle extending from the top of an object. It allows you to turn the object around—either moving clockwise or counterclockwise.

Thank you for purchasing *PowerPoint* 2003 *for Professors*. Please go to http://www.nita.org/pp4profs to download full-color, animated versions of the slides shown throughout this book. Use these starter slides to create your own PowerPoint slide shows.

Please contact NITA if you have any questions about this or any of our other publications: publications@nita.org.